DAY

TRADING

Learn the secrets of trading for profit in forex and stocks.

Suitable for beginners.

INTRODUCTION

Success as a day trader will come to only 10 per cent of those trying. It's important to understand why most traders are struggling to prevent such mistakes. The day traders who lose money on the market are losing due to a failure to either select the right products, manage risk, or follow the rules of a known strategy. In this book, I'm going to teach you trading strategies that I use to benefit from the business myself. We will first build your foundation for success as a trader by discussing the two most important skills you can possess before diving into the trading strategies. I like to think a day trader is two things, a price tracker and a risk manager. I'm going to explain how to and consistent uncertainty, and how to handle the risk so that you can make money and be correct about 50% of the time. Through putting the odds of success in your favor we turn the tables. By picking up this book, you are showing your commitment to improving your company. This alone sets you apart from most inexperienced merchants.

The act of day trading is simply buying stock shares with the intention of selling such shares, within minutes or hours, for a fee. To benefit in such a short window of time, we trade company shares that have just published breaking news, made a big earnings report, or have any sort of fundamental trigger that results in above-average retail and consumer value. Typically, the type of stock a day trader will focus on is a lot different from what a long-term investor would look for. Day traders understand the high risk rates involved with competitive stocks, and reduce those risks through holding positions for very short periods of time.

Although buyers usually search for an annual return of 5-10 percent, day traders aim for transactions that have the potential to make intraday returns of 5-10 percent. However, most day traders will take large positions to take advantage of intraday movements, which can result in a high level of single stock exposure. Some will even engage in high-risk margin trading practices (the money borrowed from your broker). A day trader with a $25k trading account, for example, may use leverage (buying power is 4x the cash balance) by sell as if he had $100k in stock. This is called to have your money leveraged. If the trader will generate 5 per cent average returns on the $100k purchasing power by actively dealing on margin, the trader can raise the original $25k equity at a pace of 20 per cent per day. The possibility is of course that the dealer would make a mistake that can cost him everything. Unfortunately, this is the story of 9 out of 10 merchants. The origin of this career ending errors derives from a risk-management breakdown.

Picture a broker who has just successfully completed 9 transactions. There was a $50 danger in each exchange and a profit potential of $100. It implies that each exchange had the ability to double the chance of a profit-loss ratio of 2:1. The first 9 active trades generate profit of $900. On the 10th sale, when the stock is down $50, the untrained dealer buys more securities at a lower price instead of taking the loss to minimize his cost base. Once he's down $100 he keeps holding and is unsure of holding or selling. The dealer takes the risk each year when he's down $1k. This is a trader who has a success rate of 90 per cent, but who is still a losing trader because he has not managed his risk. We will discuss in detail how to classify stocks and prospects for good trade, but we will concentrate first on improving the knowledge of risk management. Traders who do not use risk management strategies are expected to be among the 90 per cent of retail traders who lose money in the market.

Buying Long or Selling Short

You may not be familiar with the concept of selling short if you are new to trading. Traders who sell short borrow their broker's shares to sell those shares at a high price, with the intention of buying back the shares at a lower price and profiting from the drop. When you sell short, your account would show a negative position (e.g.-1000 shares) in your open market window. You lent and sold 1000 securities from your dealer. The broker expects you to repurchase those shares. It's called protecting your place as you buy back some assets. Many traders have a limited tendency and favor dealing of stocks falling. One of the short-selling threats is that you will eventually be forced to defend your spot if the stock goes up. Since theoretically prices can climb infinitely, if they do not cover their open short position a trader might experience an infinite loss.

For instance, if you buy stock on the long side, the maximum loss is reduced to the amount of shares you have purchased. The worst case is that the stock is going to $0. With a short position, the $5k profit becomes a $95k risk if you shorten 1000 shares of a stock at $5.00 and it goes up to $100.00. Throughout this book we will be presenting instances of momentum trades involving buying stock to the long side, but these trends could be applied equally to the opposite trend for short stocks.

Whether you're a short seller or a long biased trader, the Short Sale Restriction (SSR) is important to know about. This has been designed to reduce volatility downward and to help prevent possible stock crashes. When Short Selling Restriction is enabled on a stock, you can only shorten the stock when the price moves upwards. It prevents people from causing a recession and creating shortfalls as the price drops. SSR is switched on when a stock drops in price by more than 10 per cent compared to the closing days. The SSR is an example of a metric showing us the markets have a built-in tendency towards long-side investing. There is no such thing as a restriction on long buys. A stock can rise 100 percent, and you can keep buying as it rises. That's one of the reasons I tend to be a cynical long-term investor.

It is also important to note that there is no shorting for all inventories. The ability to shorten a stock requires that your broker has available shares for borrowing. You may not be able to short that stock if they have a small inventory.

What you Will Learn

If you've tried day trading or watched someone else day trading, you already know the concepts are simple, but it's like walking a tightrope to be successful at day trading. When you see someone do something they make it look easy, but it seems almost hard when you do it. This is the journey most inexperienced day traders are going to be going through. It's basically the same thing that I had when I was beginning to exchange. I found that the best trades are the ones with the most visible configurations and almost immediately start to work in our favor. I typically get into trouble when I and myself are in the role of keeping trades that are not working or when I start trying to force trades to work under less than optimal setups. I would encourage traders not to overcomplicate things but to focus on the obvious setups that we teach.

In this book, we'll teach you the basic concepts required for day trading. You'll learn how to manage risks, how to select stocks that are worth trading, how to identify potential setups, how to enter and exit trades, and how to manage your emotions while you trade. You are already proving your willingness to learn by taking the time to educate yourself and that puts you ahead of the majority of new traders. Some novice traders are going to trade unproven tactics, and then ask why they lose money. It's crucial that you only trade in a virtual account while you are in school. Before ever trading in a live account you will learn the tactics we teach and work on building your expertise. Throughout our live trading courses we review all our students ' results to ensure they follow a competitive trader's criteria and statistics. This implies we analyze the success levels, average loses and average wins, how much pressure they face in their transactions and how they operate under the burden of tough markets or losing positions. Once students show they can be competitive in a simulated environment, they will be ready to switch to live trading with strict restrictions on size and risk. Students in our live-day chat room trading benefit from dealing side by side with me and hundreds of other professional traders. We've educated the students in our society to be the strongest traders possible, thereby growing our trading group's overall skills.

CHAPTER 1: DAY TRADING BASICS

WHAT IS DAY TRADING?

Day trading is the act of purchasing and selling financial instruments all day long. As the day continues to progress, prices will increase and drop in value, generating both benefit opportunities as well as loss potential.

A day trader might purchase 1,000 shares of Amazon.com's stocks at 10:15am just as the price starts to rise on good news, and then sell to his customer at 10:25am when it's up by $1 per share.

It can also be explained as securities speculation, specifically purchasing and selling financial instruments within the same trading day, such that all positions are closed before the trading day closes. Thus traders who deal with profit motive in this capacity are speculators. Day trading was once a practice solely meant for financial firms and qualified speculators. Most day traders are employees of banks or investment firms working as equity investment and fund management specialists.

Day trading became popular following the deregulation of commissions in the United States in 1975, the advent of electronic trading platforms in the 1990's and the volatility of stock prices during the dot-com bubble. Some day traders use an intra-day scalping tactic that typically has the trader holding a spot for a few minutes or just seconds.

Many aspiring traders do not believe they can know a single thing. They believe they can buy software or pay a so-called expert that will place their trades for them while they're sleeping and make them rich. Or they rely on some expert's advice for their trade decisions, following his recommendations blindly without knowing anything about the markets.

Day trading is like every other business started for the soul reason for making money, you have to know what you are about to do before going into it. Definitely, with the right tools and with the knowledge to use those tools efficiently and effectively the risks of day trading can be greatly reduced. With perseverance and commitment, you can find trading success.

WHY DAY TRADING?

Whether you are new to trading or have been trading for years, putting all your faith in graphs, charts, and soft-ware is all too tempting. If merchandising was as easy as that!

The purchase of trading templates and computer programs simply does not assure your success as a trader.

Too many hobby traders attempted that and they did fail, predictably. They bought the tools, but lacked the knowledge they needed to succeed. Training, as in everything, will do wonders for the aspiring and skilled trader.

This is not, of course, to suggest that software programs and markers are not useful when it comes to day trading. On the opposite, many traders use technical indicators that are crucial to their performance–the MACD, moving averages, and Stochastic are just a few of these. However, successful day traders DO follow their metrics; they know that nothing is 100% foolproof.

You're not going to get rich in just one trade.

Successful traders know that a sure way to get burned is by trying to hit a profitable home run on just a single trade. Consistency is the key. You need to draw up a solid strategy that delivers consistent trading profits, and you have to learn and adapt as your day trading experience grows and evolves. If you want to be successful in trading, then you MUST spend both time and money to obtain the experience you need, the discipline to execute your trading strategy and the patience to wait for the "right deal."

1.) Play above the Line Playing above the line simply means taking full OWNERSHIP for all the things that are happening in your trade. Be ACCOUNTABLE for your trade choices and actions rather than trying to blame, making excuses or denying that there is a problem, and take RESPONSIBILITY for doing something about what happened.

There's no "bad market," there's just a "bad market trading strategy." No one pressures you to trade a particular market. If a market becomes non-tradable you can switch to a different market. And you can change your approach to trading so alter your trading plan. There's a lot YOU can do. As a dealer, YOU are responsible for the results of your exchange, nobody else.

2.) It can be simple to have a Positive Mindset Trading but it is not as easy as you think. Along the line, you're going to face losses, but every morning you're going to have to get up believing-in you, your strategy, and keep focused on WINNING. Ever heard of above "Law of Attraction? "Basically, it says that you need to focus and concentrate on achieving your goal in order to be successful. And the reverse also applies: if you concentrate on the negative–on losses–you will likely experience losses. That you are positive and that you are confident is extremely important.

3.) Honesty exercise this week, have you overtraded? You allow your emotions to get the best out of you? Didn't you stick to strategy? Fine, for the best of us, these things happen. But don't hide the truth from yourself and make no excuses. Be Responsible for your actions and decisions. Admit an error, learn from it and move on.

4.) Success in Committed Trading will not happen overnight. This demands your commitment, time, and effort. There are already a lot of "traders" on the market who think they know all they need to know, who think they don't have to learn anything else; they believe a "mystical system" will place their trades on their behalf and make them successful. You and I know this path to failure is a sure one.

Trading is like any other profession: you are learning the basics, you are applying them, you are gaining experience, and then you are improving your trade. Do you really expect to make billions dollars after just investing a few hours in your education? You would not trust a doctor whose only training was from free, downloadable eBooks on the Internet, would you?

No doubt: day trading can be a lucrative and exciting way to make money. You will significantly reduce the risk with the right knowledge, which will generate even more opportunities to achieve trade success.

If you're not ready to spend the time studying the trading methods, trying to read about newly improved trading strategies, and working whole-heartily in a quickly and smoothly-paced trading environment, then day trading is probably not for you.

Nonetheless, if you have the ambition, commitment and discipline, the shape and prosperity of your financial future could be seriously impacted by day trading.

Action Items:

Decide right now that you will be disciplined to follow your plan, that you are going to play above the line in your trading, that you will keep up a positive attitude, that you exercise trustworthiness, and that you are fully committed to your trading success.

Start a trading journal. Most of the successful traders around the world have one. Get your hands on a good notebook and start to record how your trading progresses and your feelings every day. You can start with that now. Write down today's purposes; you will NOT use day trading to get rich quickly. Star that three times and read it all the time. It is definitely going to help you.

WHO SHOULD DO DAY TRADING?

Trading by day isn't for everybody. Sure, there are many benefits but some "negative" factors still exist. One is that you'll suffer losses. Losses are part of our business, as a trader. If that truth is not reasonable to you, you will simply not trade. Traders who find the most success in day trading, whether in it for a living or for some extra income on the side, usually have good trading strategies and the discipline to stick to their trading plan.

Keep in mind that a very competitive sector is day trading. To succeed, you need to keep focusing on a set of strategies that you can implement without hesitation immediately. Remember, you can have an edge over the rest with a proven strategy trading plan.

Sadly, you are not guaranteed commercial success even with a tried, proven trading strategy. Something else requires. This calls for restraint.

A profitable strategy is useless without discipline. Successful day traders must have the discipline to follow their system rigorously, because they know that only trades which are indicated by that system have the highest probability of resulting in a profit.

Whether you're a new trader or have been trading for years, it's too tempting to put all your faith in graphs, maps, and soft-ware. Buying trading models and computer programs obviously does not guarantee your success as a trader.

If you want to be successful in trading, then you need to spend both time and money to acquire the expertise you need, the dedication you need to execute your trading strategy, and the patience you need to wait for the "right deal."Play Over the Line

Playing over the line means taking ownership of anything that happens in your business. Instead of blaming, making excuses or ignoring a question, be AC COUNTABLE for your trading decisions and actions, and take RESPONSIBILITY for doing something about it.

There is no "bad market," there is only a "bad market trading approach." No one is forcing you to trade a certain market. If a market is untradeable you can switch to a different market. And you can change your approach to trading so alter your business plan. You can do a lot of things. You are responsible for the results of your transactions as a dealer, no one else.

- Have a Positive Attitude: Trading can be straightforward but it is not simple. Along the way, you're going to face defeats, but every morning you have to get up believing in you, your plan and winning. Have you ever heard of "Attraction

11

Law?" Fundamentally, it means you need to focus and concentrate on achieving your achievement in order to be successful.

- Exercise Honesty: This week, did you overtrade? You encourage your emotions to get the best out of you? Didn't you stick to strategy? But don't cheat, and don't make excuses. Pay for your actions and your decisions. Admit an error, learn from it and move on.

- Be Committed: Trading success isn't going to happen overnight. On your part it needs commitment, time and effort. There are already too many "traders" on the market who think they know all they need to know, who think they don't need to learn anything; they believe a "magic machine" can put their trades for them and make them rich. You and I know this road to failure is a sure one.

Trading is like any other profession: you are learning the basics, you are applying them, you are gaining experience, and then you are improving your trade. Do you really expect to make mil-dollar lions after just spending a few hours in your education? You wouldn't trust a doctor whose only education was from free, Internet eBooks downloaded, would you?

No doubt: day trading can be a lucrative and fun way to make money. You will dramatically reduce the risk with the right knowledge, which will create even more opportunities to achieve trade success.

If you are unwilling to spend time learning the trading techniques, reading about new and improved trading strategies, and working wholeheartedly in a fast-paced trading environment, then it is probably not for you to day trade

Nonetheless, if you have the ambition, commitment and discipline, the shape and prosperity of your financial future could be seriously impacted by day trade.

Action Items: Decide right now that you will have the patience to execute your strategy, that in your trading you will play beyond the fence, that you will maintain a positive mindset, that you will demonstrate integrity, and that you will be 100% committed to your success in trading.

Start a business newspaper. It has one that most effective traders have. Get your hands on a good notebook and start trading with your pro.

IS IT POSSIBLE TO MAKE A LIVING AS A DAY TRADER?

This question is asked almost all the time by many, many people. The answer is: "Yes, it is very possible!" And, better still, you yourself can do it. Sometimes people don't accept as true when I say that they can turn out to be successful, full-time traders, but it's actually the truth. And I'm going to ascertain it to you right now.

Since I don't want to get into a lengthy discussion on "how much money is a decent salary for you," let's just say that if you were earning $150,000 a year, you'd be pretty happy, and let's say you're making this money with your trading. How does that sound? Reasonable right?

Let's break it down: $150,000 annually would be $12,500 a month, or $3,000 a week, if you prefer. It means you take two weeks of vacations a year.

IMPORTANT: When trading, don't set targets regularly. Two conditions must be met to make money:

 1.) You must be ready to trade.

2.) THE MARKET must be primed for trading.

There will be some days when you won't be at your best (illness, emotional stress, no time due to an emergency, etc.) and there will be some days when the market is not available to be traded (e.g. holidays, even days before and after holidays, days before a major news release, such as the Federal interest rate announcement or unemployment re-port, etc.).

Look at the chart below. The markets were open a day after Thanksgiving and the 24th and 26th of December, but there was hardly anyone trading that you can see displayed in the volume bar It's the same between the majority of the days after Christmas and through the 2008 New Year's Day. Despite the open markets, the volume was very thin. Markets can be easily manipulated during these types of low-volume days and could be very unpredictable, so it would be better to stay away from trading.

And that's the reason why you shouldn't set your trading goals on a daily basis: those goals will force you to trade on days when both of the above conditions–you AND the market is ready–are NOT met.

Starting small is important, and setting a weekly target for only ONE contract, or 100 shares. This target should be LOW, very low, so you can easily attain it. Think about high-jumping: you practice with a bar which is just three feet high. The jumping is easy Then, you raise the bar by another inch until you reach three feet. And another one, and another one.

You shouldn't raise the bar too high too fast to be able to trade effectively. Take it down to a level that you can handle at any time. You can always increase it at a later point in time, once you have shown you can reliably achieve your goal.

Example: You could set your weekly target at $100 per contract within the first four weeks of trading. This may sound too convenient for you, but note that 90 per cent of traders are losing money in the markets. You can start "raising the bar" if you can consistently make $100 per contract. Try to increase to the $150 per contract per week. Raise the bar over and over, but make sure you're still confident at achieving your goals.

You can use the leverage to trade multiple contracts on a rather limited account when day trading futures, options, or forex. If you're talking about trading the futures market, you will easily find a broker on a $2,000 account that will allow you to trade one contract with almost any future instrument out there—E-mini S&P, currency futures, E-mini Russell, interest rates, commodities, etc.

You could raise the bar to $300 per contract per week after sometime. And, if you're going to make $3,000 a week, you're going to have to trade ten contracts. The same thing applies to stock trading: if you can sell 100 shares for $300 a week, then you need to trade 1,000 shares to make $3,000 a week.

You may not have enough money to trade in these amounts at this stage in your trading account, but don't worry—we'll get there.

A sound trading strategy which produces consistent profits is the key element to trading success. If you can make money day trading with one contract or 100 stock shares, then you can attain a money day trading with ten contracts or 1,000 stock shares. Ideally, you'll have a high average profit per trade to attain your weekly target. The average income is supposed to be at least 50 percent higher than your average loss, preferably twice as high.

One of the approaches that I use in teaching my students calls for a profit target of about $300 per contract and a stop loss of $200 per contract. You will see that the profit target is much more greater than the stop loss. That is the beauty of day trading: all you need is a single net winning trade, and you'll have accomplished your weekly target of making $300 per contract. So if you are fortunate, you can make your weekly profit target achievable on Monday morning with your first trade.

But what if you lose?

As everybody taking part in trading knows, losses are also part of the business, and they are unavoidable. If that is something you have concern on accepting, then you should not go into trading. However, there's a significant difference between losing a huge amount of money on a regular basis and losing small in a well-ordered trading plan. You are already aware that you should keep your losses small; the goal is to keep them smaller than your average wins.

Let revisit the part I mentioned earlier: you have a trading plan that produces $300 in profits for each of your win and costs you $200 for every loss you record. Now, if your weekly target is $300, and if your first trade was at the expense of $200 loss, then you have to make two winning trades to attain your weekly profit target.

Let me talk more on this and actually break it down for you: you have lost a sum of $200 on your one losing trade, and then you make about $600 on your two winning trades ($300 each). On calculation, your net profit equals $400 which means your goal has been achieved. Now, STOP TRADING. If not, you'll end up losing the money you just made to the markets. Have strong hold on your profits!

Obviously, you're not always assured a week with only one loss. Let's have a look at a week that starts off with three straight losses. With three straight losses, you are now short of $600 ($200 each). So you would need to make three straight wins that result in $900 ($300 each). Deduct the $600 you lost on the trades you lost from the $900 you won on the winning trades, the result gives a net profit of $300. Goal achieved. Stop trading.

"Wait a moment – you are saying that I will achieve my targets with a winning percentage of only 50 per cent?"

YES! That's exactly what I am trying to say! Read the above example again: you lost a sum of $600 on three losing trades, made a sum of $900 on three winning trades, and at the end, you came out with a net profit of $300. This implies that you could pick a losing trade every other time and still attain your weekly profit targets!

I want to emphasis more on this point again, because many traders don't pay attention to this important concept of setting weekly goals. They give the daily goals, meaning, which create a huge psychological pressure, and then, if they trade their markets when they shouldn't, and they lose.

So let's assume for a minute that you end up achieving an authentic winning percentage of only 50%. Now, when you begin trading again on Monday morning, what are your probabilities of having a winning trade? 50%! You have a half chance of attaining your weekly profit target in just one single trade!

So if you DO accomplish your weekly profit goal on your first trade Monday morning, what next?

Stop your trading activity for that week! Enjoy life! It does not get any better than that.

Recall, you need to stay disciplined to your trading plan and your weekly goal. Do not go into another trade once you have already attained your weekly goal; the odds that your second trade may be a losing trade is quite high, and you would be losing your money and profits to the market after winning. Overtrading and insatiability are a trader's downfall, so fight them and stick to your strategies.

Now, you are aware that you can attain your weekly profit goal with a winning percentage of 50%. During the course of this book, I will assist you in getting an even sharper edge in your trading, generating a trading strategy with an even higher winning percentage.

A Quick Recap:

The first big move towards financial success is to state your weekly profit target. Next, you will need to find a dependable, straightforward trading plan that will help you attain your profit goal. When you go into a trade and your trade gets to either your profit goal or your stop loss, exit that trade straightaway. Stick to your trading strategies and plans until you attain your weekly profit goal, and then give yourself a break until next week.

If you have a recap on the case I gave at the beginning of this section, in order to generate $150,000 per year, let's assume a 50-week year and two weeks of holiday – you would need to make $3,000 per week. At a profit of $300 per trade, this simply means that you would need to trade about ten contracts (or 1,000 shares). Of course, this analogy can be applied to various amounts. If you wanted to make a profit of $225,000 per year with a weekly profit target of $300 per contract, for instance, then you would have to trade fifteen contracts (equivalent to 1,500 shares), and so on, and so on.

If you do not have an active trading account that makes you trade the amount of contracts or shares that I'm mentioning here, then now is the best time to start building it. Remember, be of patience with your trading, be slow, be smart, and be steady. Success in trading doesn't happen overnight, but with the right plans and structure, you can achieve encouraging results in a much shorter period of time than you may ever think of. Strategize your trades and trade your strategies. That's how prosperous traders make money.

CHAPTER 2: GETTING STARTED

HOW TO GET STARTED: DEFINE YOUR GOALS AND MAKE A PLAN?

Lots of first time traders want to jump right in with both feet when it comes to trading. Alas, very few of those traders are successful; successful trading requires knowledge, skill and experience.

You need to determine what your goals are before you dive.

- What do you hope to accomplish with your business? Why would you like to trade?
- Buying a new sports car?
- Buying a bigger house?
- To raise $100,000 annually/month /week?
- Financing a college education for your kids?
- Will produce a full-time income to support the whole family?
- Free choice of what, where, and with whom?
- To have a fun and exciting life full of outstanding experiences?
- To work less with your loved ones, and spend more time?
- Or do you just plan on making some extra cash on weekends?

Always think about what you hope to achieve with that investment, before you exchange a single penny. Understanding what your target is will help you stay focused when faced with a tough trade spell, and it will help you make better investment choices along the way.

But be realistic: Too often, people begin day-trading with hopes of instantly being wealthy. I won't say it's impossible (because it's possible) but let me warn you that it's very rare too. A trade strategy that will allow your account to develop at a slower pace over time, which can eventually be used for retirement or education of a child, is much safer to build.

So let's talk about identifying your priorities and drawing up a plan for your day-to-day business.

Here are the three key steps:

1.) Define your **SMART** goal: **SMART** is an acronym which stands for:

- **S**pecific
- **M**easurable
- **A**ttractive
- **R**ealistic
- **T**imeframe

Luckily, when it comes to day trading, identifying a target that meets all those requirements is very straightforward. Just decide exactly how much money you want to make with your day trading every month.

Example:

With day trading, I want to make $10,000 a month.

Is SPECIFIC? – Actually, $10,000 is a specific dollar amount.

Is this MEASURABLE? – Definitely! Just check your trading account balance early in the month and at the end of the month. The ac-count balance is the best way to measure the target attainment.

Is this ATTRACTIVE? – That depends on you. $10,000 is definitely attractive to some-one who currently makes $4,000 a month, but it wouldn't be appealing to someone who's only paying $10,000 just for his 6,000 square foot home in mortgage payments. Make sure that this goal motivates you.

Is this REALISTIC? – In the previous chapter, we spoke about this. Successful people believe unrealistic goals do not exist; only unrealistic time -frames. Your trading account may not be large enough for you to realistically trade enough shares or contracts to achieve your long-term trading goal right now, but if you follow the steps outlined in this book, your long-term goal WILL become realistic in the near future.

Does it have a TIMEFRAME? – You want to make $10,000 a month, of course; the timeframe is 30 days.

2.) Make a **Plan**

Developing a strategy is crucial to your success, but we get a little bit ahead of ourselves. In the second part of the book, "Your Trading Plan–The Cornerstone to Your Trading Success," we will talk about your trading plan in depth. Just make sure that you don't confuse the order: first you identify your trading objectives and then you create a trading plan.

Many traders first look for a trading strategy and then hope the trading strategy will help them reach their goals. That is putting the cart before the horse.

Whatever you do, you should first define what you want to achieve, and then plan how you can achieve that goal. Otherwise you might find out right at the very start that you started climbing the wrong ladder.

3.) **Execute** the Plan

It is here that the rubber meets the road. Once you've got your plan, you'll actually have to execute it. And, of course, that is where most of us fail.

Let me set an example to you:

Amazon lists 18,361 "Weight Loss" books and 28,707 other "Exercising and Exercise" books. That's a total of 47,068 books on the famous "How to Lose Weight" subject (compared to only 4,463 books in the "Stock Trading and Investing" category).

How to get started - define your goals and make a plan?

If I wrote a weight loss book, it's going to be very, very short:

1.) Eat less.

2.) Allow more exercise.

Come on, it's simple: we all know that if we just follow those two rules we can lose 10 pounds in 10 weeks!

We decrease our calorie intake to 1,500 to 2,000 calories per day, and then we do at least three a day aerobic exercises for at least 30 minutes.

We have a **SMART** target ("lose 10 pounds in 10 weeks"), and we have a strategy ("eat less and exercise more"), so why are we continuing to purchase these books and magazines that promise a new diet, a new way of weighing?

Since, we struggle to enforce our strategy.

And then we blame the plan: "it's too hard," "it's impossible," "it's not working." We were not successful simply because we were too lazy or we did not have the discipline to execute our strategy. But instead of focusing on the real problem-the implementation-we are modifying the strategy itself, hoping there will be an easier way.

Successful individuals will realize that their problem lies not in the plan but in the execution.

Here's what you can do to ensure your own motivation and discipline when executing your plan: Focusing on the big picture is important. It will help you stay motivated when you're learning reaches a plateau, or when there are a few losses you face. All great achievements begin with great vision.

Tell yourself this once you have established your SMART target and the amount of money you want to make from trading: "How would this goal impact your family life?" and "how would it affect you personally?"

Take the time to answer these questions and write down the answers.

Humans, as you know, are great at procrastination. We don't like being in our comfort zone and that's why sometimes we don't do anything and just "hope" that we're going to achieve our goals. As you can imagine, the odds of doing nothing to achieve a goal are slim to none. So, a-sweeping out the next issue will help you take immediate action.

Tell yourself, "Why are you supposed to act now?" If you really take the time to think about the answer, it's going to be a huge motivator. Little tricks like this will help you stay focused on your long-term goal, helping you achieve your strategy.

HOW MUCH MONEY DO YOU NEED TO GET STARTED?

This question's answer depends on the market you want to trade. In the course of the next few chapters we will use a systematic approach to determine the best market for you, but the information below will give you a basic idea of your options:

- You need at least $25,000 in your trading account if you want to sell stocks today.
- You should have between $5,000 and $10,000 in your trading account if you want to trade futures to-day.
- You should have between $1,000 and $5,000 on your trading account while selling options.
- If you are talking about trading forex, then your trading account will start with as little as $500.

Financial considerations are always important, but don't make the com my mistake of allowing your current financial situation to dictate which market you will trade. Remember: first, you define your goal, then you plan how to accomplish it.

If you don't have enough money to trade the markets you've outlined in your goals, then start to do something about it now—save more money or spend hours overtime. There are many ways to make a few more bucks, and it's better to wait for the money you need than to start trading in a market that's wrong for you and your goals.

For those of you already in your savings account with the right amount of money, let's talk about the issue, "**How much should you trade**?" Many first time traders believe all their money should be traded in. That is not real! You must first decide how much money you can sell, how much you can potentially afford to lose, and what your financial goals are.

Let's start by finding out how much of your money will remain in your savings account. It's important to keep living expenses in an easily accessible savings account for three to six months, so set aside the money and don't trade it! You should never sell the money you might need right away. Unless you have assets from another source, such as a re-cent inheritance, the remaining amount of money is likely to be what you have to deal with at present.

Look at how much money you can afford to trade at the moment. You don't want to borrow from other parts of your life when you tie up your money in a deal, so make sure you consider the original purpose of these savings.

First, decide how much you will be able to add to your business in the future. You can continue to receive income if you are currently employed, and you can expect to use a portion of that income over time to develop your investment portfolio.

Something more important to remember:

As outlined above, some types of investments need an initial amount of deposit to begin. This does not mean you risk the entire amount (see the "Determining Your Risk Tolerance" chapter on page 27). Most traders would lose just 10 per cent of the initial deposit. Never borrow to trade money, and never use money you can't afford to lose!

WHAT YOU NEED TO BEGIN TRADING?

You're going to need:

- Computer
- Internet Connection

- Charting Software
- A Broker
- A Properly Funded Trading Account
- Good Trading Plan

A COMPUTER

You don't need the new computer, and the most costly you don't need. Essentially, every machine you've bought over the past two years is going to do the trick. Many charting applications and trading platforms run on Windows, so make sure the program you're considering is MAC compatible if you're thinking about getting a MAC. Notebooks are all very well, too. Just like a checklist, the minimum requirements here are:

IBM or IBM compatible Pentium IV-class 1 GHz or higher Windows 2000 computer, Windows XP 256MB RAM (use 1GB of RAM when running Windows XP) CD-ROM drive Minimum 3GB of hard disk space.

You will need a second screen too. For the entry and exit signals, you should have your charting program on one computer, and your trading platform-form on another screen to enter the orders. A second display costs between $150-$250. Don't be cheap on monitors; make sure you're able to see your charting applications in crystal-clear detail. A 17" display is going to do the trick. A 19 "would be even better. It's pretty much overkill for 19. You can have a bigger computer, but you need not have one.

INTERNET CONNECTION

Don't be greedy on this. Don't ever try to trade using a dial-up or your phone-connected modem. A reliable Internet connection is key to your success in trading. After all, the data you collect from the market is what you are going to base on all your trading decisions, so you can't afford a pause. Invest in a cable or DSL connection. No link needed to T1.

CHARTING SOFTWARE

Online day trading has developed to the point where charting software is an indispensable tool of both professional and novice day traders alike. The times when you drew your own charts in a notebook using quotes from the morning newspaper are long gone. These days, powerful charting software packages allow you to access the market information in real-time; this information is displayed in a variety of ways, all of which can help you in carrying out your trades.

It is a very personal decision to choose the "best" charting program–it can be compared to choosing the right vehicle. What another trader wants, and vice versa, may be different from what you choose. This is why it is critical for you to carefully review a list of features–with both advertising benefits and disadvantages–before making a decision on a data feed and chart bundle. The bottom line is you need a list of criteria, and you need to use that list to compare and contrast the available charting packages. Based on the results make your choice. Here are some examples of criteria that you might wish to use:

I.   **Real-Time Data:** You need a solid platform which can immediately deliver data in real-time. That feature alone will eliminate many of the options available, as there will be some form of delay in many web-based program. You cannot afford to deal with a pause when it comes to day trading and/or swing trading, even if that delay would be perfectly acceptable in the long-term market.

II. **Market Data Coverage:** Search the markets which the charting program covers. Some packages include the big U.S. markets, but if you need other international markets, such as Asian or European markets, then you need to ensure data is available in real time.

III. **Wide Variety of Indicators:** You might be interested in a wide variety of indicators and charting techniques, such as bar charts, point-and-figure charting or Japanese candlesticks, depending on your individual needs. Furthermore, test to see whether the charting program can easily view simple indicators such as MACD, RSI, and Moving Averages. If you are serious about technical analysis, make sure that without too much trouble you can program your own indicators or modify the existing ones to suit your needs.

IV. **Competitive Rates and Money Back Guarantee:** You need tools for trading that won't cost you all your money before you even start your first company. Shopping around is necessary. Finding a competitive rate does not, however, mean the product of the vendor is the cheapest. You have to be cautious about this one—when it comes to trading, the old saying "you get what you pay for" certainly applies.

V. **Weigh the Chances:** You don't want cheap trading software that offers you next to nothing, but you probably don't need the most expensive package-you won't even use features-either. And make sure the provider you select allows you time to test how the software platform actually functions. You should be able to claim a refund within the first 30 days if you're uncomfortable with using it.

VI. **User Friendly Platform and Complete Training:** You need to have a platform that you can use quickly, not one that requires a degree as a Computer Engineer, unless you are a professional programmer. Trust me there are those kinds of platforms out there! You will need software to allow you to check back strategies and program custom indicators and trading systems without much trouble. Alternatively, if you just don't seem to be able to find user-friendly trading software out there, then find a software platform with a comprehensive user guide. A guide will help you get to know the system, and at the same time teach you.

VII. **Reputable Company:** Choose a reputable company whose platform and data feed has a proven presence on the Internet. And of course, choose a business which has excellent customer service.

Keep in mind that this list may include certain requirements dependent on your trading objectives, such as the ability to switch rapidly between various timeframes. As I said earlier: this is a very personal choice that you alone can make. The following section provides my own professional analysis of a couple of major software packages:

- **eSignal**

The eSignal (www.esignal.com) is owned by Interactive Data Corporation and has been around for more than 20 years in the trading sector. It was released over the Web in April 1999. Effective since February 2008, eSignal prices range from $125/month (for eSignal Premier) to $195/month (for eSignal Premier Plus), which makes this package slightly more expensive than a number of other trading platforms-forms out there. If you're a dealer in futures, you'll be forced to see 1,000 icons through a set of evaluating options. In other words, each month you can expect to pay just as much as $249 to $360.

Nevertheless, provided that the charting of eSignal and the data feeds come from the same vendor, there will be no issues that the software provider will blame on the data feed, or vice versa. (This' blame game' is something that every experienced trader has–or will–face when using trading software at some point.)

In my experience, the user interface of eSignal isn't the most elegant available on the market today; consumers often need to return to the help system again and again. However, the charts can be customized according to your needs in many different ways, and once you get used to the various shortcuts, the charting platform is actually pretty effective for quick decision making.

The company provides complete audio and visual training for new customers when it comes to a demonstration program. There's no need to dread being a fresh user-bie, you'll be able to get to know the app in no time.

Now, you can save this format and apply it to other charts without delay after you set up a chart in a way that you're comfortable with –which is done by customizing sizes, colors, indicators, etc.. The collections of maps and quotation lists can be stored as' Pages,' so flipping between these pages can be made quick and easy.

Every window on the portal can be accessed from the main eSignal pane, which is a tremendous help when it comes to detecting the signal.

Best of your Multi-Monitoring Systems. In addition to the charts, eSignal also provides quote lists, level 2 screens, and news tickers to keep you updated. All those features can be linked to each other. For ex-ample, choosing a symbol in a quote list will almost immediately change all the charts connected, level 2 displays, etc., to the same symbol.

All standard technical indicators are available, and there is also a program that uses JavaScript language called EFS (which is the basic language for eSignal Formula Script) to write your own series of cedures; these procedures can be used repeatedly throughout the program life. EFS can also be used to communicate with broker interfaces, and back-testing, of course.

If you really want to get into a more sophisticated configuration, there are a few tiers of API that are available at extra cost, and these provide direct access to the eSignal data feed. A regular subscription requires you to track up to 100 symbols, the next step up to 250, and if that isn't enough, you can pay a little extra to get even more tracking symbols.

The data feed itself is definitely eSignal pack's strongest element-age. A trusted global data feed for the market, on which eSignal has staked its well-known reputation in the active trader community, is available right before you. The organization operates entirely automated ticker plants to insure nonstop processing and flawless data consistency, and data can be transmitted via a flat file for you to open in Excel or another spreadsheet program.

Without a question eSignal is one of the best data feeds you can find on the Internet. For most traders, the charting commodity is efficient enough, with EFS contributing to its performance.

- **TradeStation**

TradeStation (www.tradestation.com) has become the top choice for hundreds of thousands of high-rated traders around the world since its introduction in the online trading environment in 1997; it has received numerous honors from business magazines, including Barron's and the Technical Review of Stocks and Commodities. It was also called Reader's Favorite by Stocks and Commodities Magazine Best Trading Technology Winner for five consecutive years, from 1994 to 1999. When it comes to the mapping applications-it is generally accepted as industry standard.

TradeStation is probably the world's first trading platform that provides you with the ability to create, test, and fully automate your own rule-based trading strategies every day. When you are ready for your first trade, TradeStation can automatically monitor your trading rules and even execute 100 percent of your trades.

It is also designed to help you discover some potential market opportunities and then perform your business more professionally than you have ever been able to do alone. TradeStation primarily tracks the stocks on the Web for you to tick by tick, in real-time, and searches for all the opportunities depending on your business plans.

The moment an opening occurs based on your specific buy or sell laws, it's designed to generate your entry and exit orders instantly and deliver them to the market within fractions of a second of market movement.

TradeStation has even developed a programming language named Easy Language which is very user-friendly once you get the hang of that. You may easily create your own laws of exchange, for example when to enter the market and purchase, or when to get out and sell. Practically all of the trading strategies you might ever know about can be streamlined, like multiple orders, inputs and exits, benefit goals, security stops, trailing stops and more.

It helps you to check back, configure custom indicators and adjust the Indicators to suit your needs. Then it will back-test your strategy on up to 20 years of authentic, intra-day market data with just a single click of your mouse, giving you the simulated results. TradeStation would give you information about all the trades you'd have done, your estimated net profit or losses, and much more, before you even lose a penny from your real trading assets.

When you first set up TradeStation, you can consider using the app a bit overwhelming. For $99.95 to $199.95/month, though, which helps you to use the award-winning functionality of TradeStation, it is Perhaps worth your time to get professional and familiarize yourself with this trading site. It is certainly no coincidence that TradeStation, through its stability and the strength of technology, has become one of the most popular trading platforms for active traders, both experts and novices.

- **MetaStock**

If you enjoy using the Technical Analysis Tool, MetaStock (www.metastock.com), Equis International's (Reuters bought Equis) could be your #1 trading device. And if you don't know anything about technical analysis, but always wanted to apply this kind of approach when it comes to your savings, then you might be interested in using this program as a learning tool.

MetaStock is accessible as of February 2008 at a one-time fee of $1,395. You can use QuoteCenter, which directly collects real-time data from Reuters-the world's leading provider of financial news information-and merge it with MetaStock Pro. The main program itself is very user-friendly, so familiarizing yourself with all its functions, even if you're a novice, is quite simple. The software is also fully compatible with Microsoft Office, so you can easily cut and paste data into Excel or Document.

Equis has provided all forms of chart shapes and features; by simply clicking and dragging the cursor, you can navigate trend lines, moving averages, tension lines, support lines and numerous other instruments of exchange. You can also pick the Internet alternative for collecting quotations, reports, and option symbols directly from Reuters, without charge.

The new version, MetaStock Professional 8, incorporates all the features of the previous version—such as detailed charting and visualization—and is designed to work with a Data Broadcasting Corporation real-time data stream, such as BMI or Signal Online.

Many traders say the search facility is one of the best features at Metastock. The search facility would allow you to scan the whole stock and shares inventory based on the criteria you defined. The aim is to discover any securities that show up in line with your trading strategy. The software determines then how much money you can make using a single trading strategy. The results will give you detailed information, such as when to buy and sell at what price, and how much of each trade was made or lost.

Equis can also provide you with a CD full of historical data from which to build maps, along with the online connection that you need to update the database whenever you want. You will receive a Technical Analysis manual of 550 pages, from A to Z, which will enable even the novice trader to master the methods of software and technical analysis in no time. Not to mention that there's even an interactive visual tutorial in the' HELP' menu so you won't get bored!

- **Genesis Trade Navigator**

Trade Navigator (www.genesisft.com), the trading platform built by Genesis Financial Technology, Inc., is an integrated tool for charting, technical analysis, and execution. Used in conjunction with many trading strategies, Trade Navigator can use indicators such as Moving Averages, Seasonal, ADX, and Stochastics to turn into a perfect, real-time automated trading in-instrument. Functions like Single-Click Trade, Calendar, Indicator, Bracketing, Trailing Stop and more are right at your disposal.

The interface also contains OHLC, Candlestick, Wall, Hill, HLC, Histograms, and Points and the maps can be broken down into tables. Panes can carry either specific indicator or test, or even a mix of the two, enabling you to modify the look of each chart by simply clicking and dragging your mouse to create, rotate, shift, or extend trend lines, help and resistance lines, and other items. Therefore, regardless of what display options you want to use, Trade Navigator is the perfect tool for you.

The Trade Navigator Platinum can use Tradesense, a basic input language that does not allow you to be a specialist in computer science to use it, to do all the back-testing, production and research for your trading strategies. It comes with a complete video training collection, free training and a handbook. Tradesense is the core feature of the Platinum program, and you can understand this quite easily. This blends traditional English with basic symbols of math for efficient interpretation and critical inputs.

With Tradesense, you can take any tactic concept–whether from a trading book, a lecture, or even a buddy–and check it using a range of order types (such as limit orders and stop orders) to improve and evaluate its efficiency. Tradesense can identify the markers you are searching for and fill in the values for you automatically.

Furthermore, Precision Tick is another unique feature of the Genesis testing system; it enables you to back-test any strategy and ensures that each rule is executed precisely on the basis of real-time market conditions. You can also build your next bar orders. Every plan that you bring into the system can be accomplished with a "Order." Once certain conditions, whether long or short, have been fulfilled, it will enable you to impose a specific order.

You can build your own personalized markers and tactics with Trade Navigator, you can trade directly from the map, and you can use Instant Replay mode if you want to trade. Speaking of which you can go back to a certain date in the past with Instant Replay and observe the data as it fills in, watching the way it moves on the days the bars were created.

It's like having your own time machine that allows you to travel back in time and then move on to the present time as you watch the chart change before your eyes. Instant Replay mode is the perfect tool for traders of any sort to prepare for real-time trading without any harm.

There are three different versions of Market Navigator: Silver, Gold, and Platinum. Prices start at $99 with data upgrade fees for stocks of $25 a month, or you can choose a $65 a month bundle for stocks, futures, indices, and some options. Genesis helps you to use hundreds of pre-programmed metrics and criteria so you can easily identify the best strategy based on your methodology to help you operate the software instantly.

Genesis also has a variety of training videos available, and regularly offers free webinars to help you make the most of their software package.

Charting Software Conclusion

I hope you get a better idea now of what kind of trading software will best meet your needs. Remember, powerful charting software gives you the speed and ability to perform almost instant trades in response to breaking news. You might want to move on to more sophisticated software in time as you become more experienced in the world of trade.

Note, don't buy trading software by evaluating all of the available options. If you don't take the time to compare and contrast, you might get tricked into inexpensive software that doesn't have the capabilities you need; OR, you might get suckered into expensive software that has tons of functionality you'll never use. If you need help setting up your trading platform, or have any other concerns, you can always use customer support from the business. Benefit from the free trials and money-back deals. Note, it is a very personal choice to pick the right software for you and you won't know if it's correct for you until you try it out.

A BROKER

You may wonder if you need a broker, really. Answer is yes. If you're going to sell today, you'll need to have a dealer. And whether you're exchanging bonds, futures, forex, or options doesn't matter: unless you're a member of the market, you're not going to be able to put your orders with-out a trader.

Stock-, futures-, and options-brokers are required to pass various tests to get their licenses. Such checks insure the broker understands his company and can help you as appropriate.

Understanding the difference between a broker and a market analyst is really important. An investor analyzes the financial or futures market practically, forecasting what it will or won't do, or how particular securities or assets will do. There is a trader who will follow the orders to either buy or sell, not evaluate the stocks.

Brokers often earn their money on sales commissions. If the broker is told to buy or sell, they receive a set percentage of the sale. A flat fee per contract is paid by many brokers.

Two styles of brokers exist: full-service brokers, and discount brokers.

Generally, full-service brokers can provide multiple forms of securities, can provide investment advice and are usually paid in commissions.

Usually, discount brokers don't give much guidance or research; they just do as you are telling them to do, without all the bells and whistles.

Therefore, when it comes to brokers, the biggest decision you have to make is whether you want a full service broker or a discount broker.

If you're new to invest, you may need to go with a full-service broker and make sure you make smart investments. At this level they will sell you the expertise you need. Nevertheless, if you're already acquainted with the sector that you want to sell, then all you really need is a discount broker to do your business for you.

For most experienced traders, selecting the right broker can be a boring fight. Today there are more than 100 online brokers and more choices are becoming available all the time.

The problem is too many choices selecting which broker is right for you among the many options out there is not easy.

Nonetheless, this segment is all about giving you the required tips to find an ideal trading broker.

First of all, if you are searching for a forex trading dealer, you will need to increase your vigilance. Because the foreign exchange market is worth trillions of dollars, it offers traders lucrative opportunities to set up their businesses digitally. And as the foreign-exchange market is decentralized, it can be difficult to identify quality brokers with fraudulent practices among all unscrupulous brokers.

If you follow the guidelines below, your chances of finding an honest and reliable forex trading broker will dramatically increase: Always ask for references that you can actually speak to.

Check with local regulatory agencies and make sure you are registering the forex trading broker. For brokers based in the United States, see if they are registered with the Commodity Futures Trading Commission (CFTC) as Futures Commission Merchants (FCM), and registered with the National Futures Association (NFA).

Compare the account details, such as minimum required balance, interest, spreads, etc. Specifically ask them if premiums, lot payments etc. are chargeable. This is to insure that hidden costs are sustained. Many sly brokers may purposely give you the impression that they are the easiest to use, but in reality, when it comes to hidden charges, they can reach you where it hurts.

The trading platform has to be simple to use. Many traders find it challenging to navigate the trading software, especially first-timers. It can be a struggle to just make sense of the maps and the currency values. So, if demo accounts do exist, try them.

I also included a list of questions in the Appendices for you to query your broker.

Note, when it comes to making you a rich citizen this broker or company will be your partner. So be careful and be picky.

A PROPERLY FUNDED TRADING ACCOUNT

Clearly you need to exchange in currency. But you've seen this message countless times as well: "Don't deal for capital that you can't afford to lose." You would believe this is just the usual caution that every trading business specialist has to use. But this is not true. There is much more to it.

Let me give you an example: a few weeks ago, I received an email from a trader who told me that his wife had issued him a deadline: if he did not sell profitably within the next four weeks, he would have to stop trading entirely and get a' real job.' I'm not suggesting that the wife of this trader had no ground to stand on, however, as you'll know in the third part of this book, there's more to practice than that. You've probably heard that the two greatest enemies of a merchant are terror and greed. This is the case quite often. That's why con-it is extremely important for your trade to troll your emotions.

So, imagine the situation this trader is in for me. For the next four weeks He MUST be competitive every single week. Would you think as he enters into a trade he'll be cool and relaxed? Can you believe he regulates his emotions? Do you believe he can hold to his trading strategy and schedule if he fails a lot of trades?

Instead, do you think he's going to be scared of losing capital, which means giving up everything he LOVES to do? When he gets hit with more and more defeats it will probably be hard to hold to a schedule or policy. Don't you think it's pretty likely he's going to start making bad decisions and, essentially, start playing his money in the markets, hoping for wins?

I can't stress enough the importance of not putting too much pressure on yourself or your performance in trading. Yet you certainly shouldn't quit your day job just yet to keep the pressure to a minimum. Your performance needs to be consistent before you become a successful day trader and your results should be almost regular. Give yourself enough time to prove you have what it means for a living to trade in.

As for the exact amount of money you like, it depends on you. Too much capital can be just as risky as getting too little liquidity in your trading account. If you have $100,000 in your trading account and pay just $100 per trade, you may think of your losses as peanuts. Although we have to learn to accept losses as part of the business, we should never think of them as peanuts! There is balance. They've got to find something.

Therefore, to avoid situations like the aforementioned trader, he got him— himself in, appropriately fund your account— not too much and not too little. And be prepared for a period of time in which you may not be making much money with it. As with everything, when it comes to business, there is a learning process.

A TRADING PLAN

Last but not least definitely: you need a good trading plan. You can have the new device, six cameras, a T1-Internet access, the world's best trader, and a well-financed trading account, but none of these can give you trading profits. NEVER begin trading without a plan to sell.

You'll learn how to build a successful trading strategy that works for you in the next part of this book.

Action Items: Check your computer to see if the minimum requirements set out in this chapter are met. If not, decide how much the update to your machine would run. You don't have to upgrade your computer-or buy a new one-now, but if you're getting ready to trade, you should know the cost.

Test the current Internet service and decide if need be the expense of an update. Same as with the other trading elements: no need to update now, but you're going to want to know the cost once you launch your trading.

Look at various software packages for the charting. Many give a 30-day free trial. Get to know the software, and make a decision based on the software's "ease of use," NOT the price. Nearly every day you will be interacting with this app, so it's important to choose one that suits you best. You don't want to spend a lot of time learning the software-when you start your trading career. It would have to be intuitive and easy to use.

Start calling several brokers to get quotations. Brokerage is highly competitive, so for the right fee you need to look around. But as outlined above: do NOT purely base your decision on commissions. Your broker is your only member of the team and you want a member of the team that you trust and that knows you. Try to find a "close broker" in a call center that has a direct line, and does not "cover." Ask him what he is able to offer you. You'll get the impression of being a "healthy" broker after a few calls.

CHAPTER 3: RISK MANAGEMENT

One of the first items I mentioned to you was that day traders are market hunters, and risk managers. We are going to debate risk management in this segment. As an aspiring day trader, you are already aware that day trading is one of the most risky investment techniques. Instead of making more conventional, longer-term investments, the explanation traders prefer today's exchange is because day trading will deliver even larger gains in a faster time period. Day trading, when done properly, is one of the best ways to grow a small portfolio. The problem that people aren't going to deal properly. Successful traders can use $25k accounts to produce more than $50k a year, or 200 per cent of dividends. Nonetheless, for a broker to use a $250 million account to deliver $500 million per year wouldn't be practical. The markets do not typically have the liquidity to support a trader entering or exiting a multi-million-dollar position within minutes, but positions of tens of thousands or even hundreds of thousands of dollars can be executed almost immediately. This allows day traders with accounts below $1 million and as low as $25,000 to use leverage and high-speed trading techniques to generate significant percentage gains. When a trader reaches a point where they manage more money than they can day-trade efficiently, they would typically start branching out by adding longer-term investments to diversify the portfolio.

Whilst recognizing that day trading is one of the highest risk investing strategies, our attention is caught by the opportunity for a big reward. We should agree there will be relatively higher risk day trading strategies and relatively lower risk day trading strategies within the field of day trading. Our goal is to build a trading strategy to optimize the potential for profit while taking steps to minimize harm. Each time you sell, you have to calculate the trade danger and balance it against the incentive. Often times our emotional state or previous trading experiences can cloud our judgment. If we've experienced a loss recently, we may decide to take more risk on the next trade to offset the previous loss. Or a more cautious trader may decide to cut back on place sizes or even miss good trade opportunities because they lost money the last time they traded that configuration. This requires an enhanced level of self-awareness to know when making clear choices regarding danger compensation and when our judgement becomes clouded. This is a skill learnt over time. By journalizing while you trade, you can develop a sense of mindfulness and then review your notes after the market is closed.

DIFFERENT TYPES OF RISK

There are a couple of different types of risk that you need to understand when we talk about risk. We are primarily concerned as day traders about the difference between our entrance and our stop (the amount we would exchange for a loss). Your stop loss should be based on a recent chart support or resistance region and should always remain below your estimated loss number for the currency. Most of the losses we're experiencing will be when a trade drops and hits the stop price.

The second kind of risk that we need to be aware of is market volatility. We enjoy uncertainty as day traders but it also poses a challenge since extremely volatile markets will result in greater losses than we originally planned for. Because we realize there is a continuum of ambiguity in day trading, at times of extreme uncertainty, including breaking news, we choose to stop day trading. As news comes to fruition, individual stocks or the market at large will move in a broad and unpredictable range. Instead of running into the sector during that uncertainty phase, we are waiting for the dust to settle until we assess a possible business advantage.

The third type of danger is the chance of you being revealed. Exposure shall be calculated by multiplying the share price by the number of shares that you hold. As an investor, you need to be factoring in the risk of exposure because long-term positions are retained. Usually, an investor will not commit more than 10 per cent of the portfolio to a single stock. Day traders use leverage, by comparison, can encounter particularly high rates of exposure risk. While this level of risk has to be carefully monitored, by holding shares for short periods of time, most day traders can mitigate this risk.

STOCK HALTS

Stock holds are a form of risks that can be a nightmare for day traders utilizing broad positions. The exchanges can stop trading at any time. There are different types of product stoppages. There are market-wide supply stoppages that only arise when the exchange involves a technical glitch or some sort of computer error. Such stoppages can last a few minutes, hours or possibly longer. Those are uncommon. The more common stock stops are stops of volatility and stops pending material news release. It can restart at a much different price any time a stock is halted. The risk is that a stock may reopen far below the maximum amount you lose. By understanding what causes halts, we can take certain steps to avoid stoppages. The market has created what is termed circuit breaker stops. The market can be suspended for five minutes if a stock rises or falls more than 10 percent in a 5min time. This is a break in uncertainty to offer markets a chance to get their focus, evaluate data and slow down. This is a measure to prevent situations with flash crashes. These types of halts can be fairly common in volatile markets. Often times when some type of company news is leaked it can lead to a quick move and then a halt in volatility. They often open higher when stocks are stopped from going up. Conversely, they often open lower when they're stopped from going down. If sales are stopped awaiting reports, this means the company is reporting important content data. Once the news is published, the stock is set for reopening. The stock rising open significantly lower if the news is bad. That is one of the biggest trading risks. Stocks that may be halted awaiting reports contain stocks that are rapidly rising for no apparent reason. In these cases, it is not uncommon for the company to issue a statement about the price action, or to address the rumors that the price action may cause. While stocks can be stopped at any time pending news, when the market is closed, news is typically released.

The form of stock halt popular with penny stocks but not as frequent with higher priced stocks is a halt pending investigation by the government. This is typically the result of the market manipulation and theft using a warehouse. Stocks can be suspended for weeks or even months, pending an investigation.

As day traders, we need to be mindful of market stoppage risks and restrict our positions on stocks at risk of being halted. High risk inventories include penny stock stocks and stock trading on unconfirmed reports that the business itself has not published. This can happen, in spite of our strongest efforts to avoid getting stuck in a pause. That is one of the reasons margin trading can be so risky. If you're stuck in a pause and the stock declines by 20 percent, if you're selling on the edge, it could lead to a massive loss or even a margin call from your broker.

A DAY TRADERS STATISTICAL ADVANTAGE (2:1 PROFIT LOSS RATIOS)

I would be taking extremely large risks when I was a young investor without any real understanding of the level of risk I was facing. Without a predetermined maximum loss, I would enter trade and if the trade went against me, I would become paralyzed by fear. I couldn't think or make a decision, as I'd watch the loss grow bigger and bigger. The first error was entering a trade without outlining the risk versus the reward first. I would often buy stocks as an illustration, because they hit whole dollar rates. So I could buy 1000 shares of a stock at $8.90 with the goal to sell it at $9.10 for profit of 20 cents. Unfortunately, I would often keep until the stock fell below the closest half dollar of $8.50, when the stock pullback. I'd gamble 40 cents in this case, to earn 20 cents. This is a negative amount of profit loss that takes an accuracy rate of 66 percent to break even before commissions. That's not a viable ratio, especially for a new trader. I didn't know anything about profit-loss ratios when I was a young investor, so I kept doing those uneducated trades and then asking why I was losing money. Using a net loss ratio of 2:1, my correct exit should have been $8.80 rather than $8.50. I could justify taking that trade with a 10 cent stop and a 20 cent profit target. Which implies which my correct stop was just 25 per cent of the damage I faced as an untrained dealer. This is an enormous difference! It implied that I could potentially reduce my risks on these kinds of transactions by more than 75% by using appropriate risk management. It is incredibly important to understand because, regardless of your approach or the configurations that you deal, any transaction has the ability to double what you are at danger. If you don't have the potential to win twice the amount you're losing, you shouldn't accept the deal. You have set yourself ahead of the majority of new traders by simply understanding profit loss ratios and the huge statistical advantage of a profit loss ratio of 2:1.

DATA MINE YOUR TRADE HISTORY

If in an excel folder, you're not already monitoring all of your transactions, I suggest you start doing this now. The details that you want to monitor is the setup kind, period, mark, size, entrance, exit, quantity made, sum lost and notes. I have been tracking all of my trades for so many years and have the benefit of being able to review thousands and thousands of trades. I will arrange my data according to the plan, the profit or loss, or the time of day. I dig into my trading performance analytics to get a deeper insight into where I have strengths and where I need to make adjustments. When you know, for example, that the bulk of your earnings are in the morning, and that your biggest losses are in the afternoon, you will continue to become more vigilant during afternoon trading. You can also keep track of your monthly profit-loss figures and always work to improve your numbers. If you trade 500,000 shares every month and you can increase your average profits by 1 cent per share, your profits will increase by $5,000 per month. This shows you that, at the end of the month, very small adjustments in your statistics can lead to huge differences. That also illustrates the walking requirements of the tightrope merchants. The disparity between success and failure in your ratios may be the subject of a slight adjustment. The aspect that is easier to manage about your profit-loss ratio is your total loss.

CAPPING YOUR LOSSES – BE VERY GOOD AT BEING WRONG

If I speak to a trader who has experienced a major loss recently, I like to spend time analyzing the exchange which resulted in the loss. I often start by asking the trader what they were at risk when they went into the exchange. A beginner trader rarely enters a position which intends to risk as much as they ultimately lose. That is the first mistake. We have to learn how much we lose every time we participate in a transaction. It means understanding the logical place where the product should be sold for a loss if the pattern or system falls. Before we get into the patterns of the chart and the definitions of exit indicators, we will first say that when they hit our maximum loss, we stop all trades. Sadly, there are many traders entering position without thinking a total risk.

Every business plan should have a maximum loss per transaction, and a maximum loss per day. We propose that students adjust their daily total loss to their goal for daily benefit. If they have a profit target of $200 per day, if they are down $200 the day they shut down their computer and walk away. While it's hard to accept failure, it's much more important to realize that once you've reached your total setback, your decision is almost sure to compromise. Walking away is always safer, rather than trying to trade in a weakened emotional state. Much as we get a maximum loss per day, so we also get a maximum loss per transaction. I typically set my maximum loss at around 25 percent of my daily target. When I take a deal and immediately the market flips against me I take the loss. Over the years of working with students, I've noticed that some students take their defeats very well, while others fail to push the sell button. Some are transforming just short-term day trades into long swing trades. I should consider setting automated stop orders with your broker if you are in the category of traders who frequently find themselves over your pre-determined total loss. If the price falls below the stop limit, the request will be executed immediately and you prevent clicking the Sell button yourself. Although this element of trading management can be challenging to turn over to the machine, it is sometimes the best technique for students struggling to take the losses early. While trading, it's important to remember that irrespective of how you traded last week or last month, this is your chance to prove to yourself that you can follow the rules and conform to your trading plan. If you want to survive as a merchant, it is of paramount importance that you are able to keep to the laws of maximum loss per contract and maximum loss per day. Essentially, this means walking away from the computer as you reach your daytime limit deficit, even if it's rough.

Day trading is a profession where you can commit a catastrophic mistake, and then try to sell moments later. You could take a share place of 30,000, risk $15,000, and then do it another five times in a row. You might easily blow up your entire portfolio in just one day, and a couple of trades. Such type of event is the result of an emotionally fueled transaction. In allowing yourself to walk away after reaching the maximum loss, you will avoid the temptation of getting into a loop of losing and trying to make up for your loses. For example, if you crash your car into the wall, you're finished with the race in other careers and have to wait until the next race. The very nature of that kind of job gives you a time to reflect on the mistakes you made that led to the accident. Trading day doesn't come with these built-in periods of time out after we make a mistake. We need to incorporate them into our trading plan as they are extremely important to our emotional development as a trader. When we are in a heightened emotional state, they are what prevent us from making mistakes.

BALANCING YOUR RISK

When you take 10 trades a day and gamble $100 on the first nine trades and then risk $1,000 on the 10th selling, it doesn't matter if you have a success rate of 90 percent until you lose the last trading. You're going to become a loser investor. That's a risk management element called balancing risk. You never want one deal so strongly loaded with fear that it has the ability to delete past winners. Even if the final trade had the potential for profit loss of 2:1 (risking $1,000 to make $2,000), it is a poor decision, because the risk of one trade far outweighs your average trade risk. Most traders, including myself, would change our performance-based risk per exchange throughout the day and respond to higher market conditions. This is a common practice used on days where trade is successful to increase profits, and on days where trading becomes bad to minimize losses. The distinction is that in smaller increments I'm managing danger so the impacts of winners or losers won't have a strong effect on my overall performance. When I lose $100 on the first six transactions, I the decide to increase the risk to $150 or to lower the risk to $75 on the seventh, but in the middle of a trading day I would not make a drastic change to my risk criteria. There will be a wonderful day for many novice traders before they want to swing for the fences and take a high risk stance on what they consider is a perfect setup. When they miss out on that high-risk deal, they'll refund all of their gains from the day and eventually go into the red. This is a

46

devastating financial loss but the loss of confidence and the effect it has on the feelings is even worse. This is the kind of action that can lead a trader to quickly fall into a trap of emotionally driven selling known as vengeance trading. Trying to make up the difference fast by making ever more aggressive transactions. To order to completely escape this scenario, a trader must spread the danger across all deals, so if that final trade is a loser, it will not affect their day or their strategic influence over future trades.

GAMBLERS THINK ABOUT PROFITS, TRADERS THINK ABOUT RISK

The stock market is a location where all the diverse characters work together to transact together. You're going to find long-term buyers, institutional investors, radical activists, stock traders, and gamblers too. Unfortunately, day-trading has a negative connotation to some who find it to be gambling similar. Every full-time trader knows this is far removed from reality. A dealer makes decisions based on a plan that has context information to support it. The only way out of investing to make a career is to consider the exchange risk and follow the rules of your trading plan. Yet, there will always be those who actually play with their trading accounts in pursuit of huge profits by taking risky positions. You might just as well go to a casino if you want to compete. The odds of having a good stock trade and making a fortune are extremely slim. We can't base their plan or life on chance. Greed is a powerful emotion that can cause you to throw off your rational thinking processes, much like fear. If you ever notice the selfish feeling setting in, it's a perfect time to turn off your screen and walk away. Since we trade with and against the world's best traders, we should not be trading if we are unable to trade at our peak performance levels.

ADD TO WINNERS NOT TO LOSERS

Although there are many traders and investors using a scaling-in strategy, adding shares at different prices to get a good cost base, I avoid adding to stocks below my entry price for day trades. When I buy a stock at $10.00 and it fall to $9.50 I could double my stake and change my cost base to $9.75, but I'm contributing to a losing position afterwards. If it fell to $9.25, I'll suffer a loss twice as much as the initial loss if I just sell at $9.50. I've found the best trades work nearly instantly in all of my trading years. Occasionally, I'm able to get into a trade and it almost hits my halt, and then flips around and ends up being a winner, but more often, such trades are losers. I prefer to cut the damage instead of committing to a losing deal, and push on to the next chance. You risk making the loss bigger when you focus on adding to the losers, and you miss the opportunity to find a better setup.

By contrast, if I buy a stock at $10.00 and it goes up to $10.50, I might double my position and have a new $10.25 cost base. If the stock rises to $10.75 or $11.00 I'm going to make more with the improved stake, and if the stock drops down to $10.25 or $10.00, I will sell for breakeven or a small loss. Moving to successful deals gives you the potential for big wins while moving to losers gives you the potential for big loses. Since we want to work on capping our loses, we will avoid adding to the losers.

UNDERSTANDING STOCK PICKING VERSUS RISK MANAGEMENT

This is a good moment to remind you that as long as you have a good profit loss ratio, you can be a successful investor with an accuracy rate of 50 per cent or less. Getting successful doesn't involve getting correct on every deal, it's about capping the risks and taking up trades that offer winners the opportunity to beat the losers. I rendered the analogy of the dealer early on who loses money despite a success rate of 90 per cent. This trader may be a great stock picker but a losing plan stems from his lack of risk control. It is important to pick good stocks, but it is obviously not as critical as controlling the risk on every deal. I mention this to encourage you to focus primarily on your vulnerability and the potential loss to each exchange. We should discuss stock collection as an extension of risk management in the next segment. By trading the right stocks, we can enhance our chances of success especially when combining risk management techniques.

CHAPTER 4: YOUR TRADING STRATEGY

HOW TO DEVELOP YOUR OWN PROFITABLE DAY TRADING STRATEGY

It is not as difficult as you might be led to believe to establish a successful trading strategy. Most people are going to tell you that developing your own trading system is extremely difficult, but it is actually pretty straightforward. The next section of this book will teach you in seven easy but very necessary steps how to build your own trading strategy.

Step 1: Market Selection

Step 2: Timeframe Selection

Step 3: Trading Style Selection

Step 4: Defining Entry Points

Step 5: Defining Exit Points

Step 6: Evaluating Your Trading Strategy

Step 7: Improving Your Trading Strategy

MARKET SELECTION

With the popularity of online trading, more and more financial resources are available for trade in-instruments. You have a range of options, not just securities, options and futures. Financial instruments such as Exchange Traded Funds (ETFs), Single Stock Futures (SSF), and the Foreign Exchange Market (forex) have become available to private investors in the last years.

Therefore, the existing financial instruments have been strengthened. Ex–Changes have begun to introduce electronic contracts and mini contracts for popular commodities such as gold, silver, crude oil, natural gas, and grains. These futures contracts have become very common among day traders, and the volume of mini and electronic contracts has quickly exceeded the amount of the commodities traded in pit. Ultimately you can swap anything these days. Of example, if you want to engage in the real estate market without owning property, you can invest in real estate investment trusts (REITs), or even real estate futures of a particular area, such as Chicago or Denver (traded at the CME). In this chapter, we'll focus on the four main markets: stocks, forex, futures, and stock options. We'll examine each of these markets according to the following criteria:

1.) Low Initial Capital Requirements

Low initial capital ensures that with a low initial investment you can begin your day trading activities. Trading with small capital is always easier, and then jumping up to bigger capital when you are confident enough with the market

2.) Leverage

The second key is power. With sound risk management in place, highly leveraged markets allow us to put a small amount of capital onto the market and realize greater potential for profit. This will allow us to quickly build up a small account.

3.) Liquidity

The third factor for this is liquidity. We'll be focusing on liquid markets to prevent market manipulation and slippage issues. We want to ensure that we provide fast and accurate fills for our orders when trading a market, and also that a large order placed by a market-maker or broker does not move the market in an unpredictable manner.

4.) Volatility

Volatility is the fourth element. In any market you can make money, as long as it is moving. It is incredibly difficult to trade a market that is just going sideways and not heading in any direction. Trading a stock that either goes up or down, is better.

You will learn how to trade every market throughout the course of this book, but it certainly helps you to know something about the market that you are trading. And, at the beginning of each of the following sections, we will include a brief description of markets and participants.

TRADING STOCKS

The stock market for trading company stock at an agreed price is a private or public market. Industries get investors to offer an interest. The company's interest is split into a number of shares. These shares can be bought or sold (raising or lowering the value of the company).

If you buy stocks, you are simply buying a small piece of that business whose shares you just bought. You are going to get a partner. Therefore, the more shares you buy, the greater the portion of the business that you own. If the company's value grows, then the value of your stock increases. If the enterprise value declines, the share value decreases.

When the company makes a profit, in the form of dividends, you may get some of that profit; the profit is shared among all the people who own the stock. Share holding is normally called equity.

There are two main types of stock—preferred stock and common stock—and the ownership of preferred stock over common stock provides many advantages. Here are the most significant ones:

1. When you own a preferred stock then you are paying the dividend before any dividends are paid to common stock holders.

2. Unlike a common stock dividend, a preferred stock typically pays a fixed dividend that does not fluctuate.

3. Owners of preferred securities will have a greater claim on the properties of the company. For instance, preferred stock holders are compensated first, before common stock holders, in the event of bankruptcy.

Though, as a day trader, you don't really have to care about the different stock forms or dividend yields, as you're holding a stock just for a few minutes or hours.

Avoiding Stock Trading Scams

If you have an email account then you've already received a lot of Free Stock Trading Tips spam. Somebody suggests a "hot stock" in these emails. If you were to follow these instructions, you would likely end up getting stuck in a so-called "pump-and-dump" scheme.

Here's how it works:

These so-called stock picking services buy a certain stock that's usually trading at $0.02-$0.30. Many times, these stocks are not even listed on the exchanges, and the volume is typically only a few thousand shares per day.

After these stock picking services buy tens of thousands of these shares, they start recommending it to their subscribers. You'll find that it's not easy to buy these stocks since they're not listed on regular stock ex - changes. And, if you ask your broker to buy this stock for you, you might end up paying 4-5 times more than normal in commissions.

The stock picking service is now hoping that many of their subscribers will start buying this stock. They typically say, "It's trading now at $0.02 and it should go up to $0.12." That would be a whopping 600% increase! Since stock traders are greedy by nature, many will probably start buying this stock, and since there is a sudden demand, the stock prices will go up – initially.

But, before the stock hits the predicted exit price, the stock picking service starts selling (or dumping) the shares that they bought BEFORE they recommended it to you. Since they bought such a large amount of this stock, there's suddenly an enormous supply available again, and prices start falling. More and more investors panic and sell their stocks, which drives the stock prices even further down.

After a massive sell-off, the stock is generally trading at the same level it was BEFORE the stock picking service started recommending it. And, in some cases, it'll be much lower, resulting in a loss for whoever was drawn into the trap. So, investors are losing their money, and the only winner is the stock picking service. Here's an example of a "pump-and-dump" scheme: The following image is a screenshot from an online service that is offering "Free Stock Tips."

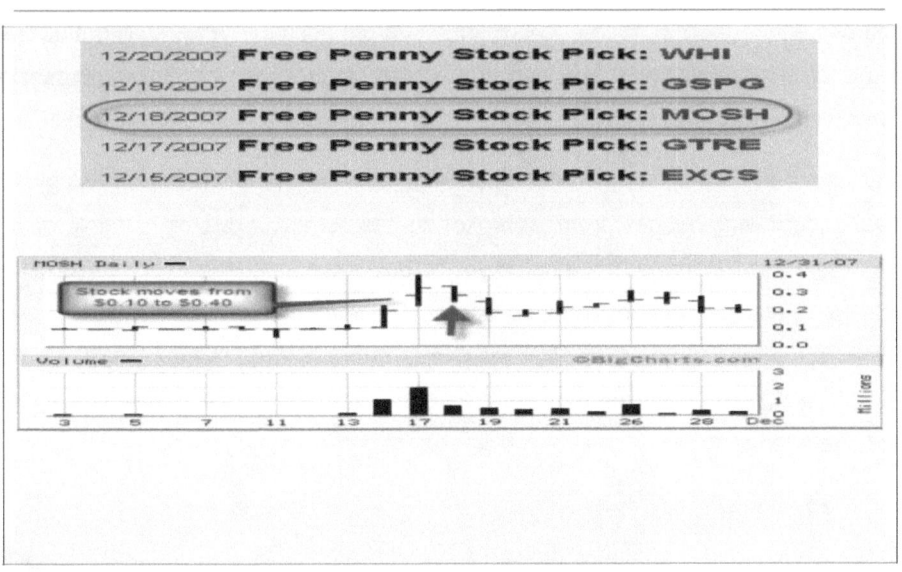

As you can see, stock prices start moving at an unusually high rate, two days before the "hot tip." You would have bought it at a price between $0.25 and $0.35 per share if you were to buy MOSH on Dec 18th, 2007, at the arrow point, as recommended by this service.

Remember that the "hot stock pick" is selling at $0.20 a few days later, and you'd have lost 25-75 per cent of your earnings.

Let's review the stock market according to our criteria:

1.) Capital Requirements

The Pattern Day Trading Rule was established by the NYSE and NASD in August and September 2001. This rule states that "if a trader makes four or more day trades within a span of five business days, then he must hold a minimum equity of $25,000 in his margin account at all times." That means that you need at least $28,000-$30,000 if you want to day trading stocks, because if you suffer losses, you need a "cushion."

2.) Leverage

You can either open a "cash account" or a "margin account" while selling stocks. While you open a cash account, you can buy or sell stock for exactly the amount that you have in your account.

You can trade stocks marginally when you open a margin account. Margin buying means borrowing money from a broker to buy stock. You might think of it as a brokerage loan. Margin trading helps you to buy more stock than you would usually be able to. A margin account requires an initial investment of at least $2,000, although some brokerages allow more. This reserve is referred to as the minimum margin. You can borrow up to 50 per cent of a stock's purchase price once the account is opened and operational.

3.) Liquidity

More than 10,000 inventories are currently available on U.S. stock exchanges. About 900 stocks are traded with an average daily volume of more than 2,000,000 shares and more than 600 of them are traded with more than 3,000,000 shares per day. If you focus on these stocks then you're not going to have a market manipulation or slippage problem.

4.) Volatility

Throughout 2007, the Dow Jones Index's average daily price change was between 1% and 2%, and many of these stocks jumped even more drastically than that:

- Alcoa, Inc. (AA) moved between 2% and 5% per day
- American Intl. Ag (AIG) moved between 2% and 8% per day
- American Express (AXP) moved between 2% and 6% per day

And that's just naming the Dow Jones ' first three companies. Volatility in the stock markets, particularly in 2007, was not a problem.

Conclusion:

Stock markets have good liquidity and volatility, but the initial capital requirements are high ($25,000) and the maximum leverage is only.

TRADING FOREX

This business may sound incredibly complex and daunting to address, but believe me, it isn't. The basic rule in the forex market, like any other form of trading, is that you have to buy when the market is going up and sell when the market is going down. The word "forex" originates from Foreign Exchange, and FX is often abbreviated. Forex trading includes the purchase and sale of currencies. In a simpler sense, it's swapping one currency at a negotiated rate for another. If you have ever traveled to another country, chances are that you have sold your currency against the currency of the local country. You have a good idea of how forex trading operates, if you've done that. The Forex market involves all of the world's currency. Choosing which one to exchange may be complicated, but all you really need to know is the big currencies, the most commonly traded ones.

Here are the main currencies:

- **U.S. Dollar (USD)**
- **Japanese Yen (JPY)**

- **British Pound (GBP)**
- **Swiss Franc (CHF)**
- **European Union Euro (EUR)**
- **Australian Dollar (AUD)**
- **New Zealand Dollar (NZD)**
- **Canadian Dollar (CAD)**

The next thing you need to know is that forex is exchanged into pairs of currencies. Trading currency pairs means you are buying one currency while selling another currency at the same time.

Examples:

Usually, the most commonly traded items are: EUR / USD USD / JPY GBP /USD

Knowing the Forex markets are extremely volatile is very useful to you. You can make (or lose) thousands of dollars in one day, quickly. Most forex brokers offer "free quotes and maps" and "no fees," but note nothing is free of charge. You pay a premium-i.e. you can't buy a currency and sell it for the same price instantly.

When you're on vacation, it's like at the exchange booths: you might ex-switch $100 to 80 Euros, but when you switch the 80 Euros back into dollars, you only get $96. The same concept applies when trading forex: you pay at least 2 "pips," which is about $20 depending on the currency pair that you sell.

The forex markets can be complex and not to be taken lightly.

Another downside to forex trading is that you're NOT trading at an exchange: there's no "Foreign Exchange." You're dealing against your broker: if you're selling, then your broker buys from you, and vice versa. And that's why the quotes are offered to you by your broker for free: he will give you* any* quote he wants because there are no regulations.

Example:

Look at the quotations from those forexes. Each three of the following screenshots were taken at 3:00pm U.S. on Tuesday January 1 st, 2007. Easter Hour.

Note: The time shown at GMT in the first two charts (+ 6 hours) I used three different websites to acquire the quotes:

Symbol	Bid	Ask	High	Low	Open	Change	Time	Favs
XAUUSD	↓833.4	↓833.9	838.9	833.67	833.84	↑0.1	02:13	Add
XAGUSD	•14.78	•14.83	14.84	14.8125	14.83	•0	14:00	Add
EURGBP	↑0.7344	↑0.7348	0.7364	0.7342	0.73477	•0	15:01	Add
EURUSD	↓1.4586	↓1.4598	1.464	1.458	1.4598	↓-0.0005	15:01	Add
EURJPY	↑162.79	↑162.82	163.42	162.5	162.747	↑0.07	15:00	Add
EURZAR	↑9.9586	↑9.9886	10.0263	9.9625	10.0031	↓-0.0145	16:00	Add
EURCHF	↓1.654	↓1.6543	1.6576	1.6393	1.6541	↑0.0002	15:00	Add
EURCAD	↑1.4494	↑1.4502	1.4601	1.4488	1.4511	↓-0.0009	14:59	Add
EURAUD	↓1.6657	↓1.6667	1.6743	1.6651	1.6662	↑0.0005	15:00	Add
EURNZD	↑1.9033	↑1.9053	1.9118	1.9029	1.90544	↓-0.0001	15:00	Add
EURSEK	↑9.4423	↑9.4463	9.4511	9.4242	9.4401	↑0.0062	15:01	Add
EURSGD	↓2.0749	↓2.1249	2.1295	2.1004	2.1046	↑0.0203	15:01	Add

Name	Bid	Ask	Change	%Change	High	Low	Time
EUR/USD	1.4586	1.4589	0.0001	0.01 %	1.4611	1.4577	19:59
GBP/USD	1.9861↓	1.9866↓	0.00↓	0.00 %↓	1.987	1.9838	20:00
USD/JPY	111.54	111.58	-0.12	-0.11 %	111.76	111.50	19:56
USD/CHF	1.1341	1.1351	0.0016	0.14 %	1.1347	1.1313	19:58
USD/NOK	5.4372↑	5.4462↑	0.0024↑	0.04 %	5.4474	5.4279	20:00
USD/DKK	5.1088↑	5.1158↑	-0.002↑	-0.04 %	5.1141	5.0989	20:00
USD/SEK	6.4687↓	6.4767↑	0.0088↑	0.14 %↑	6.4747	6.43	20:00
USD/CAD	0.9936↓	0.994↓	-0.0042↓	-0.42 %↓	0.9978	0.993	20:00
NZD/USD	0.7663	0.7671	0.0007	0.09 %	0.7663	0.7637	19:03
AUD/USD	0.8755	0.8759	0.0002	0.02 %	0.8769	0.8744	19:59
USD/MXN	10.911	10.941	-0.0046	-0.04 %	10.9156	10.894	19:02
USD/SGD	1.4395	1.44	-0.0014	-0.10 %	1.4409	1.4361	20:00

Solution by NetDania   Data Source: Comstock llc

Major Currencies - Real-Time

Currency	Bid	Ask	Change	High	Low	Time
EUR/USD				1.4748	1.4567	20:01:00
USD/JPY				112.29	111.2	20:02:00
GBP/USD	1.9855	1.9874		2.0101	1.9788	17:59:00
USD/CHF			0.0013↑	1.1372	1.1199	20:01:00
USD/CAD	0.9936↑	0.994		0.9986	0.9763	19:58:00
AUD/USD	0.8757↑		0.0009↑	0.8827	0.8733	20:02:00
EUR/JPY				165.5	162.3	20:01:00
EUR/CHF			0.00	1.6587	1.6381	20:02:00
GBP/JPY	221.52↑	221.59↑		224.91	220.84	20:02:00
GBP/CHF			0.0033↑	2.2625	2.2241	19:59:00
CHF/JPY				99.86	98.14	20:02:00
NZD/USD	0.7661↑	0.7666↑	0.0009↑	0.7794	0.7645	20:00:00
USD/ZAR	6.825	6.845	0.0255↑	6.8665	6.762	19:00:00
Gold	833.4	833.9		843.8	829.4	07:13:00
Silver	14.78	14.83	0.00	14.92	14.66	19:00:00

Look at the high of the USD / EUR currency pair this day: It is recorded by the first data source at 1.4611. The second source of data suggests 1.4748.

The third source of data recorded a high of 1,4640. That's a 137-tick gap which is $1,370! Do you see the issue? The Forex prices are wholly subjective.

MINI-FOREX TRADING

Although the capital requirements are al-ready low, "Mini-Forex Trading" has recently become very popular. Mini-forex trading is good for people who have just started on the forex market and lack the funds to open a daily account. This needs less money than standard forex accounts-a minimum of $250.

You can exchange up to 5 mini lots on that account. A mini lot is just 1/10th the size of a regular forex account.

Example: A 25-pip stop loss on a regular account equals a loss of $250. Since a mini-forex account is only one-tenth of the normal forex account, this stop loss is only $25. You sell in 10,000 units instead of dealing in 100,000 units.

What are the advantages of trading on Mini-forex?

You still get to reap advantages such as a free trading site—just like daily forex traders— even with just a small stake involved. Some more advantages include state-of - the-art trading software, maps, and services.

This way, you can build confidence in your trading skills while slowly increasing your income and market position. Until heading for the higher stakes of daily forex trading you get to manage your money on a small scale.

You can also establish a sound trade policy without involving yourself too personally in future gains or losses. For practice, newbies can begin with paper trading; they can start small with mini-forex trading in the real market.

Conclusion:

Mini-forex trading requires a smaller amount of capital and less emotional investment and it provides you with the ideal opportunity to develop your skills and trust as a trader gradually. In a way, it will prepare you for the higher stakes of the more advanced foreign-exchange world.

Let's test on our conditions for forex trading:

1.) Capital Requirements

Most forex brokers allow you to start your trading account with as little as $1,000.

2.) Leverage

The typical forex market leverage is 1:100-i.e. you can trade $100,000 for every $1,000 in your trading account. Forex traders recently began offering 1:200 leverage, allowing you to swap $100,000 for every $500 in your trading account.

3.) Liquidity

That's certainly not an issue on the forex market. Unfortunately needless to say, since the forex market is decentralized and there is no official exchange, data on the amount cannot be accessed in real time.

Nevertheless, according to the 2007 Triennial Central Bank Survey, the conventional foreign exchange market's average turnover is about $3.21 trillion a day, and it's still that. Here are the daily forex-market turnover averages over the last 15 years:

- $880 billion (April 1992)
- $1,15 trillion (April 1995)
- $1,65 trillion (April 1998)
- $1,42 trillion (April 2001)
- $1,97 trillion (April 2004)
- $3,21 trillion (April 2007)

4.) Volatility

In forex market you can find decent volatility. It's not as large as in the stock market, but due to the extremely high leverage even small movements will produce substantial profits. Here are the average daily movements for three different currency pairs:

EUR / USD — between 0.5% and 1% per day of USD / JPY — between 0.5% and 1.5% per day of GBP / USD — between 0.5% and 1.5% per day.

Keep in mind that these movements represent approximately $750 — $1,500 per day for every $100,000 traded.

Conclusion:

Forex markets are highly competitive and criteria for capital are as small as $1,000. Leverage is at least 100:1 and the volatility is decent. Overall, forex seems to be a good trading market, but keep in mind that as mentioned earlier in this section, there are some drawbacks too.

TRADING FUTURES

Trading in the future keeps growing in popularity and many traders are jumping into this type of investment. Trading futures offers many benefits, particularly if you're new to trading. Yet many traders shy away from trading in futures because they are not familiar with it.

When it comes to future, there is a lot of misunderstanding. People often think that futures are highly risky and hard to trade. That's true to some ex-tent. Futures trading IS more volatile than stock trading due to the high leverage. Yet futures trading–due to the high leverage–even pro–gives the private trader an excellent opportunity.

What are the possibilities, then? Contracts of the future, simply called futures, are ex-derivatives exchanged in transition. These are structured contracts between purchasers and product sellers that specify the quantity of a commodity, the grade / quality and the place of the distribution. Usually these futures contracts are exchanged on futures markets, such as the Chicago Trade Board (CBOT), the Chicago Mercantile Exchange (CME), the New York Mercantile Exchange (NYMEX), and others.

Below is a list of various types of Future contracts:

1.) **Currencies**–The currency market is probably the best available option, trading in the British Pound, the US Dollar, the European Euro, etc.

2.) **Interest rates**–Interest rates are traded on this market in two ways: long-term interest rates are defined by T-Bonds, and short-term interest rates are used by T-Bills.

3.) **Fuel**–A range of fuel commodities, including natural gas, heating oil and crude oil futures, are traded on that market.

4.) **Food**–Sugar, coffee, and orange juice are just a few of the regular commodities traded in the sector.

5.) **Metals**–Commodities are fairly well-known in this market, such as copper, gold, and silver.

6.) **Agriculture**–Futures include wheat, corn, coffee fees and soybeans in this region.

Futures aren't borrowed like stock, so starting a short position is as common and easy as buying the futures.

A Little Bit of History

Commodity trading started in Japan at the beginning of the 18th century, with rice and silk trading, and likewise in Holland, with tulip bulbs. Trading in the U.S. started in the mid-19th century, when central grain markets were developed, and farmers were provided a marketplace for bringing their goods and selling them either for immediate delivery (called the spot or cash market), or for forward delivery. All contract trading began with conventional commodities such as grain, meat, and cattle. These days, exchange trading has grown to include commodities, oil, currencies, currency indices, stock indexes, government interest rates, and private interest rates, too. The Chicago Mercantile Exchange launched futures on financial instruments in the 1970s. These instruments were enormously successful and soon over-in terms of trading volume and global market transparency, commodities futures took hold.

The Commodities Future Trading Commissions (CFTC), an independent United States government agency, oversees all futures trades in the United States. Each futures contract is characterized by a number of factors, including the nature of the underlying asset, when it must be delivered, the currency of the transaction, and at what date the contract will stop trading, as well as the size of the tick or minimum legal price change.

Here is a list of the five most commonly used futures contracts:

1.) **S&P 500 E-mini** –This contract has all the advantages of S&P 500 but the investment costs are much smaller. It can be traded electronically, nearly 24 hours a day, five days a week. It is gaining exceptional prominence in futures markets.

2.) **E-mini NASDAQ 100**–This contract is electronically traded as with the S&P 500; it tracks the movement of NASDAQ 100. The margin amount required for trading is substantially lower than a standard contract, and since not all traders have the funds to trade on the normal NASDAQ 100, this E-mini is the perfect solution.

3.) **Light Sweet Crude Oil**–Oil futures are among the most common commodities out there. Every time you hear in the paper or on the news about "the price of oil," this is the contract that they're talking about.

4.) **Gold**-The contract for gold futures is also popular. The United States introduced the Gold Standard in the 1970s, establishing a major position for gold in the US economy.

The gold price has been going through frequent, dramatic changes since that time and those changes are generally in the opposite direction of the U.S. dollar. The gold futures contract follows the price changes per ounce of gold, and hedge funds are often used to invest in gold.

5.) Euro FX e-mini–The Euro FX e-mini contract shifts with the exchange rate between the Euro and the US dollar. As with the rest of the E-mini contracts, the margin amounts needed to trade the Euro FX are much smaller than the normal contract rates, which means this contract provides a fantastic opportunity for traders who don't have accounts big enough to trade the regular contracts.

The growing popularity of futures trading stems from the fact that buying or selling a futures contract requires only a relatively small amount of money, called the initial margin. By definition, certain futures margins are a deposit in good faith to ensure credibility for market participants.

You must pay a small initial fee each time you open a position by buying or selling futures. The downside is that the initial margin on a potential stock is much lower than the cost of acquiring the current stock outright.

Example: The graphic below shows an actual stock index, the S&P 500.

The index may rise from 1560 to 1570. It is trading at around 1561.80 as of 12 October 2007. Many people think that buying the entire market index is less risky than having an individual stock. The stock exchanges thus created an artificial stock called the SPY (also known as the SPYDER contract).

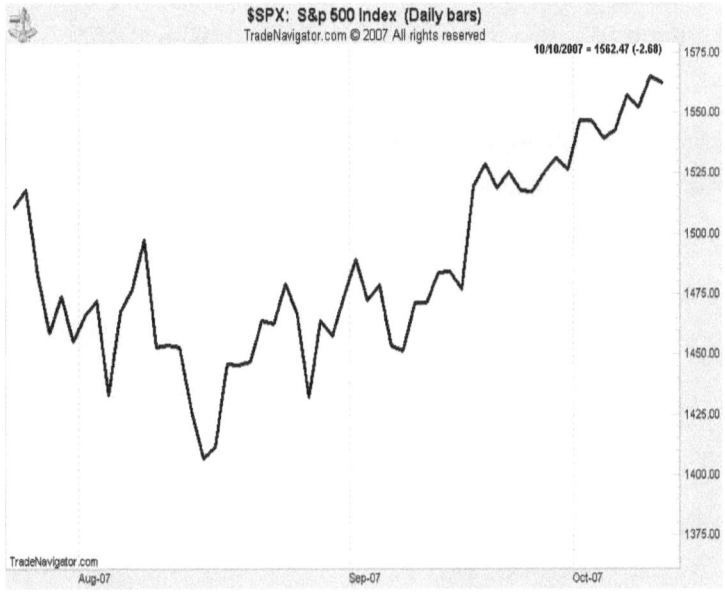

In reality, the SPY stock mirrors the S&P 500 Index, but usually you can't trade the entire index. If you wanted to trade the entire S&P 500 index, you'd have to buy all 500 stocks in the index, literally. Clearly, something you can't do. The SPY is divided by ten, to make it affordable for private traders.

So, we are monitoring the index, and a factor of 10 decreases the artificial stock—it's trading at 156. If the SPX (the index) moves between 1560 and 1570, then the SPY moves between 156 and 157.

When you swap one SPY share, you'll make or lose one dollar. And how much capital is needed to get one share traded? 156 Dollars.

So for 156 dollars, if the entire index drops by 10 points, you'll be compensated with a one dollar profit.

In addition, if you were trading 500 shares of the SPY, then you would make 500 dollars on a move of 10 points. Obviously, the capital needed for 500 shares is much higher than for one share. The capital needed is actually 156 dollars per share times the 500 shares that you would want to trade.

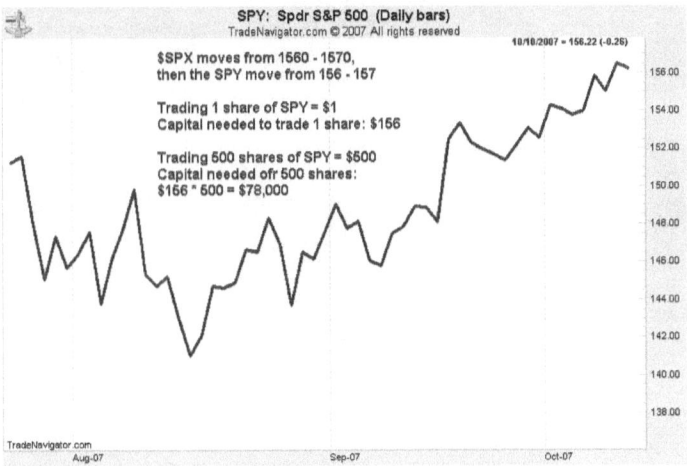

The total capital needed to trade 500 shares would be $78,000.

It's pretty much $78,000. The thing to look at here is your investment return, which is what the majority of traders use to measure their success.

If you make $500 after investing $78,000, the return on that investment would be 0.6%. That's a very small amount in the underlying index, for a 10-point move.

That's precisely why we have the stocks for the future. In the futures markets, there is a massive advantage because you only have to invest a relatively small amount of money (the initial margin).

Below, the following chart shows the so-called E-mini S&P Futures contracts:

You will see that the E-mini is much closer to tracking the index–here we are looking at a current value of 1574.50. The important thing to know is that if the E-mini S&P moves from 1560 to 1570-which is also abbreviated as ES-you will actually make $500 per deal.

And how much of an investment is needed in this move to make $500 off one contract?

About USD 4,000.

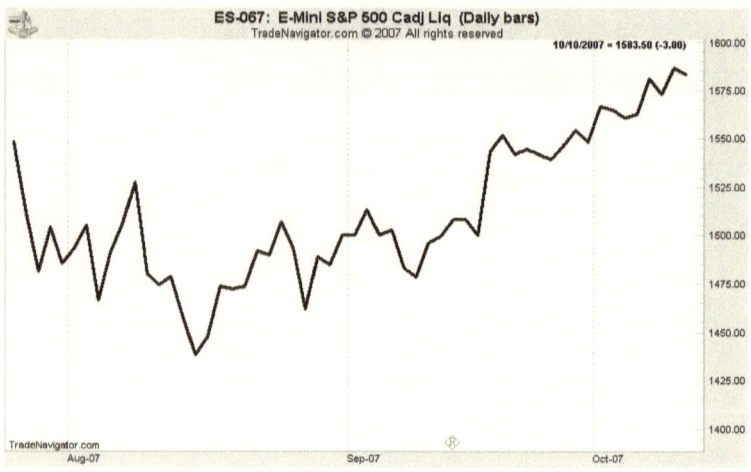

The margin requirement for the E-mini S&P is roughly $4,000. And if you're trading it on a daytime basis, you'll even get a discount, meaning that you'll only have to pay $2,000. It's even as lit sometimes like $1,000.

So, for a benefit of 500 dollars you can deposit 4,000 dollars and participate in a 10 point transfer. Let's calculate our initial investment return on that.

We're looking at 12.5 percent instead of 0.6 percent. That's more than twenty times the return that you'd get using the SPY contract.

That can be a double-sided knife, of course. You can easily make $500 but if the trade goes against you, you'd lose $500. And, in fact, trading one E-mini S&P contract is no different from actually trading 500 SPY shares.

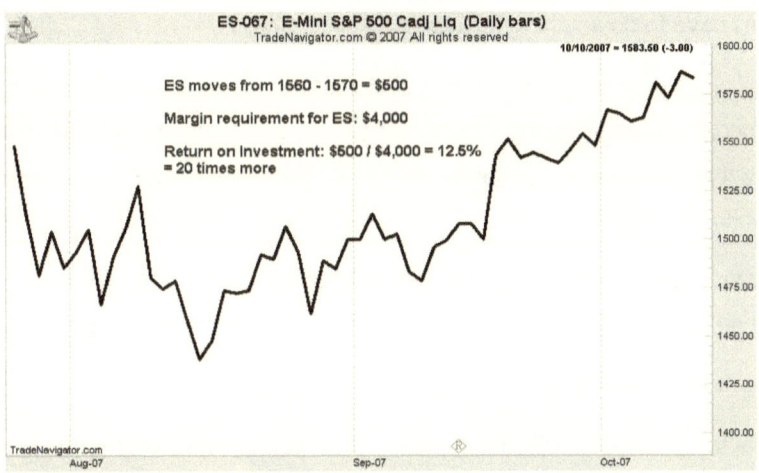

The Futures Trading Myth

As you can see at the bottom of the preceding table, small Rs exist. Such Rs state the dates of expiration. A futures contract is valid only for a given period of time. For the E-mini S&P, a contract for the futures is valid for 3 months. This term may be learned from choices. There's also an expiration date for Options.

A new futures contract begins trading after expiry date and the old contract expires. You might have heard horror stories that you will have to take delivery if you hold a position and the futures contract expires. According to these stories, if you transact the crops, such as maize, and the contract expires, you will get the delivery of cornered to your doorstep.

Yes! For yes! That wouldn't happen!

Essentially, what will happen is this: your broker will get in contact with you and give you some details before the Futures contract expires. It'll probably be something to the effect of, "Sure, this futures contract will expire in a couple of days ' time. We should get rid of or roll over this position. "Rollovers are when one contract expires, and the other contract actually begins trading. It is something that will be taken care of by your broker, so you don't have to do anything at your end.

Believe me, your broker has no interest in getting you a physical delivery of corn, you have no interest in getting a physical de-livery of corn, and it's doubtful anyone else will be interested in getting you a physical delivery of corn either. Yeah, don't believe those horror stories.

 Just get your broker available and you shouldn't have any issues. Make sure he has a number where you can be contacted so he can let you know what's happening.

A Little More On Futures

Let's go back to the S&P 500 Index. As you can see by the decimals in the following graph, it's trading at one-cent increments.

It has been simplified even further to make futures trading a little easier. If you look at the following example, it is trading in quarter increments on the very right hand side. If the E-mini S&P futures contract moves from 1560 to 1570, you are going to make or

68

lose 500 dollars, depending on what position you have taken. And if a move of 10 points converts into a gain or loss of $500 then a move of 1 point is worth $50.

The minimum tick movement (or mini movement-mum movement) is a quarter when trading the S&P e-mini. You can see, therefore, that it goes from 1550 to 1550 and a fifth, 1550 and a half, 1550 and three quarters, and then up to 1551 If the minimum movement is a quarter then a total of $12.50 (one quarter of $50) for each tick shift. Quite facile. For one case, there are four quarters, so you just have to divide the 50 dollars by four.

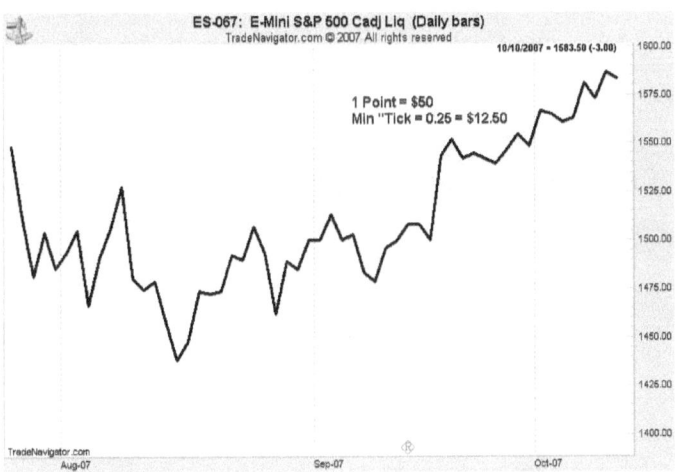

Why is this important, then? Okay, it's not really–all you need to know is that you can make a return of 50 dollars per point if you swap one futures contract with anywhere between 2,000 and 4,000 dollars. Keep in mind that you can lose $50 per point too.

Note, the $2,000 to $4,000 we're talking about is the initial margin, which is the sum of money that a customer like you have to deposit with the brokerage house for every futures contract you buy or sell.

Now, just think about it for a minute: let's say you have an account of $80,000 what can you do with it? Okay, you could buy up 500 SPY stock shares. Or in the ES, you might trade 20 futures contracts. If you choose to sell the 20 futures contracts rather than the 500 SPY stock options, you'll make $10,000! If you stick to the SPY shares, you will only be making $500 per 10-point move.

You can see the distinction. On your ac, you get a much bigger leverage-count with futures trading, and a higher leverage is exactly what will allow you to expand your account (as long as you know what you are doing).

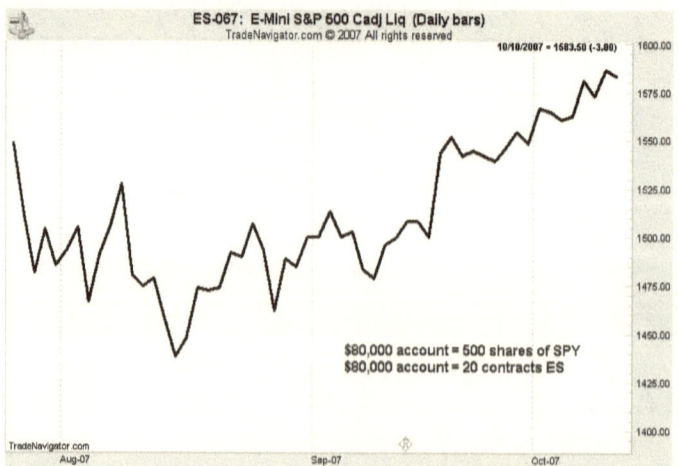

Margins and Accounts

There are 2 margin forms. The initial margin (sometimes referred to as the original margin) is the sum of money that the buyer will deposit with the brokerage firm for each purchase or sale of a futures contract. All buyer and seller shall pay initial fee.

Additionally, for each open contract, the maintenance margin is the minimum amount that an investor must always hold on depositing into a margin account. Maintenance margin is typically smaller than the original margin. For example, assume that the initial margin needed for buying or selling a particular futures contract is $2,000. A possible cost for marine gin repair could be $1,500

Another important thing to be aware of when working with margins is what is called a call to margin. If the margin drops below the margin maintenance condition set by the futures listing exchange, a margin call will be given to get the account back to the level necessary. Essentially, you should expect a margin call if you need $1,500 in your account for your open contracts, and you don't, otherwise.

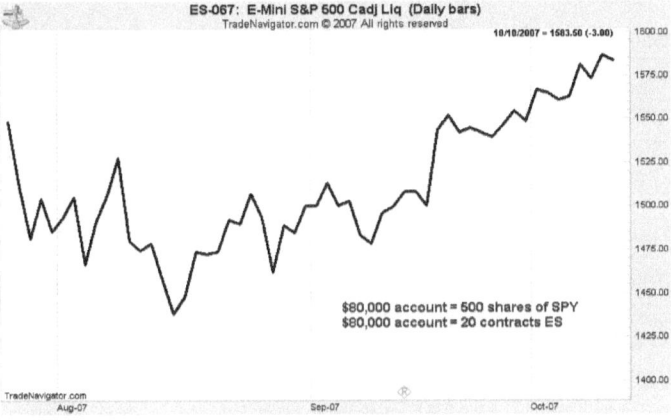

The difference between futures trading and stock trading is that the portfolio is settled regularly. Every day that earnings accrue on your open positions, the profits in your margin account will immediately be added to the ledger, not just when you close the place. If you buy stocks, all the money you make or lose will either be added to or subtracted to your account only after you close your spot.

Therefore, as gains take place on your futures contracts, they will be added to your margin account balance and losses will be deducted from your margin account balance on any day.

Keep in mind that if the funds remaining in your margin account fall below the maintenance margin requirement, your broker will require you to deposit additional funds to return the account to the required margin level. Once, that's called a call to bottom. A future trading gives everyone an equal opportunity to make a profit even with a small bank account, due to the low margin requirement.

Pros and Cons of Futures Trading

A future trading is among the most heavily leveraged and potentially profitable financial activities of today. It enables traders to create their own accounts fast, but if you take futures trading lightly, as stated earlier, you could also wipe out your trading account within a matter of days. Therefore, it is crucial for your trading success that you train yourself diligently in futures trading, and only trade with a proven and solid trading strategy.

If you're new to futures trading, deciding which contracts to actually trade can be especially difficult. There's a lot of choices! Probably the best way would be to start with the more common goods, until you get a better idea of which contracts suit you and your company the most.

The more you know about the fundamentals of such futures contracts and commodities, the better your chances of successful trading. Let's look at futures trading according to our criteria:

1.) Capital Requirements

You will need to deposit an initial investment into your futures trading account to trade a futures contract. As of writing this book, most potential brokers need a $5,000 minimum, though I've seen some brokers able to open an account with as little as $2,000 as possible.

2.) Leverage

The leverage depends on the futures contract that you are selling and the value of the contract. An initial mar-gin is required for every contract. Here are some examples for the most common contracts (as of January 2008):

- E-mini S&P–as low as $500 to trade in a $75,000 contract (Leverage 1:150)
- E-mini NQ–as low as $500 to trade a $45,000 contract (Leverage 1:90)
- E-mini Gold–as low as $400 to trade a $27,000 contract (Leverage 1:67.5)

3.) Liquidity

Also, the price depends on the contract you are dealing in for future. Here are a few numbers:

- E-mini S&P: approximately 2,500,000 contracts / day
- E-mini NQ: approximately 500,000 contracts / day
- Euro Currency: approximately 200,000 contracts / day As you can see, the liquidity varies, so you must test the amount of the futures market you intend to sell.

4.) Volatility

For futures markets you'll find decent volatility. The high leverage, as in the forex markets, would allow you to make good profits, even if the markets move only a few points. Here are some average daily fluctuations:

- E-mini S&P: between 1% and 3% per day
- E-mini NQ: between 1% and 2.5% per day
- E-mini Gold: between 1% and 2.5% per day

- Euro Currency: between 0.5% and 1.5% per day

Keep in mind that those movements reflect approximately $500-$1,500 per day for each contract traded.

Conclusion:

Future markets can be very liquid, and requirements for capital are as low as $2000. Leverage is at least 1:50 and the variance is good.

Future markets are regulated, and usually the spread is 1 tick (mini-contract movement mum). Committees usually are less than $5 per transaction. It's no surprise that for their trading efforts, many day traders choose the futures market.

Make sure you check the market volume and liquidity you want to trade, as there are enormous differences between markets.

TRADING STOCK OPTIONS

Trading stock options is quite similar to trading futures–both involve buying stocks at a fixed price, and then selling them when the price rises above its original amount. You have the right–but not the duty–to buy (call) or sell (put) a particular underlying asset at a pre-arranged price on or before a given date when you purchase an option.

Example:

Suppose you buy a call–a right to buy–100 ACME Holding Inc. shares at an agreed price of $40 per share (strike price) on an agreed date in March 2008 (expiry date) and pay $5 for the option.

When ACME Group Inc. were trading on–or before–the expiration date at less than $40 per share, then you would not be exercising your right and you would have lost the price you paid on that option-$ 5.

But if ACME Holding, Inc. trades at $50 per share on or before the expiry date, then the right is actually worth $10. This is the difference between the price at which the right to buy ACME Group, Inc. is priced at –in this case, $40–and the price it currently sells for – $50.

The opposite of that is an option for putting (right to sell) on an underlying asset. At present, you can believe the market is overheated, and you want to buy a put option (right to sell).

This will grant the person who bought the put option the right to sell the option on or before a specific date (expiration date) at an agreed price (strike price).

TIMEFRAME SELECTION

When day trading, you're naturally going to select a date that's under one day. Popular intraday periods are 60 minutes, 30 minutes, 15 minutes, 10 minutes, 5 minutes, 3 minutes and 1 minutes. Generally, the average earnings per transaction are relatively low when you pick a smaller timeframe (less than 60 minutes) On the other hand, you are getting more chances to trade. The average profit per transaction will be higher when trading on a longer timeline, but you'll have fewer trading opportunities.

Smaller timescales mean lower income but also typically lower risk. If you start with a small trading account, you may want to select a tiny timeframe to make sure you don't over-leverage your account.

Nonetheless, you can experience a lot of "noise" generated by hedge funds, scalpers, and automatic trading when choosing a very small timeframe like1-minute,3-minute, or5-minute. You may think you're seeing an emerging trend just to realize it's only a quick orchestrated step and the trend is over as soon as you get into the market.

Hence, I suggest using charts of 15 minutes. This timeframe is small enough to catch the fun intraday fluctuations, but it's large enough to minimize the noise on the market and show the "real trends" correctly. You should always experiment with different timeframes when designing a trading strategy. A technique of trading that does not work on a small timeline may work on a broader timeframe and vice versa. Start developing your trading strategy using 15-minute charts and adjust the timeline first before adjusting the entry or exit rules if you are unhappy with the results.

Action Items:

Start your trading plan on page 245 and pick an initial timeline under "Timeline Selection."

TRADING STYLE SELECTION

You need to determine, after choosing a market, which trading approach you want to use. The main question is whether you are going to use simple or advanced analysis-sis to determine which method to trade, and when to enter and leave.

FUNDAMENTAL ANALYSIS

Let's look at the definition of fundamental analysis:' Fundamental stock analysis requires, among other things, a close examination of the company's financial statements to determine its current financial strength, future growth and profitability prospects, and current management skills, to estimate whether the stock price is undervalued or overvalued.

In other words, fundamental analysis is the study of fundamental, underlying factors affecting the supply and demand of the contracts being traded in. The root cause of market movement is investigated in fundamental analysis.

You can find a snapshot of some' main numbers' for IBM in the graph below. In addition to this company-specific data, you need to take into consideration the overall economic climate and start looking at different macroeconomic indicators such as levels of economic growth, interest rates, inflation rates and unemployment.

Interest rate hikes, for example, are rarely good news for stock markets. This is due to the fact that, when there is an increase in interest rates, many investors will withdraw money from a country's stock market, causing the currency to fall.

It can be tricky to know what effect prevails. The Dow Jones Index fell 300 points when the Fed reported an interest rate cut in December 2007. As the Fed cut interest rates in January 2008, the Dow Jones Index soared 200 points.

In addition, economic reports with key data such as PPI, CPI, PMI, GDP, and, recently, even housing statistics, have shown considerable stock market effects.

Confused? If you don't have any sense with the abbreviations and the "key statistics" on the graph below, or if they confuse you, you're not alone.

Basic analysis isn't simple. That is why most market analysts have some economic background, both in macro-and micro-economics. Big trading firms like Goldman Sachs hire economics experts with Ph. D.s and you shouldn't be trying to compete with them.

Even if you decide NOT to trade stocks and want to focus on futures or forex markets, then you still need to look at crop and weather reports (if you're trading grain futures), interest rates and the country's economic data (if you're trading forex), or follow developments in the Middle East and the status of pipelines and refineries worldwide (if you're trading energy fuel).

TECHNICAL ANALYSIS

Here's how it defines technical analysis:

"The basic principles or assumptions of technical analysis are that the current price of a stock reflects all available information on the market, that price movements are not random, and that pat-terns in price movements tend to repeat themselves or trend in some direction, in very many cases. Technical analysis also includes analyzing stock trading trends through the use of charts, trendiness, support and resistance rates, and many other statistical analytical tools to predict future stock price movements and help identify trading opportunities.

In summary, a technical analyst applies three main points:

- Market action discounts all. Whatever the fundamentals say, the price that you see is the price that you get.
- A given security's price moves on trends.
- A security's historical trading patterns will tend to repeat itself.

Both three of the above points are relevant but the most crucial is the first. It is vital that you understand this point, because it is the foundation of our trading approach. Looking at the price of any financial instrument as a technical analyst, you believe it's the true value of the product as the market sees that. For a couple of reasons I believe in the technical analysis.

The markets are driven by greed and uncertainty, not offers and demand. The economic report as such is meaningless: it is the reactions of traders to the data that moves the economy.

Price data is more "objective." Whatever you want, you can view financial data and economic reports, but support levels are support levels, and a high weekly is a high weekly. Hard facts can be interpreted more easily than financial statements, because many times these statements may be misleading.

Example: IBM reveals that it will miss the projected sales targets, and the stock would drop like a rock, as traders hoped IBM would go beyond its goals. Another day, DELL announces that they will meet their targets, and the shares will jump up, as traders did not believe that DELL would make it because of the "difficult economic environment." Learning technical analysis is easier (and therefore faster). You can learn the basics by reading a few books, whereas to master fundamental analysis you need to study micro- and macro-economics. And even then, the market could fool you.

An Example of How Fundamental Analysis Could Fool You

The March unemployment rate was published on Friday, April 7, 2006. The market was expecting a 4.8 per cent unemployment rate, and the numbers came in better than expected.

Only 4.7 percent. This is good news, aren't they? The market should be rising upwards, right?

FALL! The E-mini S&P had dropped 20 points that day. Why? For what?

Okay, here are some quotes from a news service: "Not surprisingly, the March employment report dominated equity trading on Friday. More importantly, it was the reaction of the Treasury market to that that set the stage for stocks."

"A lack of negative surprise caused the stock market to breathe a sigh of relief." "The Treasury market had a very divergent reaction to the data, and with that it took down the stock market. To Treasury traders, the in-line data essentially did not provide any proof that the Fed would be willing to end its currency tightening cycle early. "Oops. So stock traders thought there was good news and the market was moving up, but the treasury trader in the other room thought the unemployment report was bad news. The problem that will be battled back and forth: "Are sky-high oil prices reflective of a slow-down or impending inflation in the economy?" And more importantly: How will the Fed respond? Will they stop raising interest rates or lower the rates yet again? That would give stock market a boost.

Alternatively, will traders fear an economic slowdown that could result in lower earnings for the company? This would drive the demand downwards.

As you can see, it's not the news that drives the market-it's the traders ' reaction to the news that causes prices to jump up and down.

Using a technical approach, you don't have to strain your mind to justify why the economy is behaving as it is. You simply assume the factors affecting price — including economic, financial, and psychological factors— were all integrated into the price you see.

It means that the market participants have already factored into the current price anything that can affect the price of a financial instrument. Technical analysts look at charts the same way a doctor looks at x-rays: they analyze the charts for details about future market direction.

DAY TRADING CHARTS

If you're new to the game of investing, and you're not a Ph.D. in Economics, then charts are the way forward. The Bar and Line charts are the most common charts. Indeed, even if you are an experienced trader, bar and line charts are likely to still have a special place in your daily life of trading. Clearly these charts are important.

"A picture speaks a thousand words." For charts this proverb holds just as true. Charting is the visual representation of the actions of a financial market over a period of time.

Each market has four different trading points over a single day. They are: opening price (O), closing price (C), actual daytime high price (H), and the day's absolute low price (L). All these points are shown on the charts.

The opening price (O) represents the day's first trade. Individual traders tend to place orders when the market opens, in response to the closing of the day before. Typically, this price will be based on emotional judgments and might well suggest how the first half—or the whole day's trading—would turn out. The closing price (C) is the most recent exchange of the day. In general, it is institutional investors who place orders towards the end of the day. In comparison to the opening price, the closing price would usually be indicative of justification and analysis does not gut instinct.

The low (L) of the day and the high (H) of the day are rather self-explanatory. On the maps, the difference between the high and the low is called the Scale. The fifth variable shown on a chart is usually the volume (V), representing the number of shares, lots, or contracts exchanged over the time between the market open and the closing. It will not be enough to plan future trades just to look at these five points on the maps. To evaluate market trends, you need to look at them over a number of periods.

Day traders use trading charts to track the markets they sell, and decide when to do business. There are several different types of trading maps, but all of them display basically the same details about trading, such as past and current rates.

We will address the three most common forms of trading charts in the section below.

BAR CHARTS

A bar chart, also known as a bar graph, is a chart of rectangular lines, the lengths of which are equal to their size. Bar charts are used to compare two values, or more.

The bar chart is one of the most common methods of charting. A bar graph shows a single bar extending from the high to the low of the trading period it is intended to depict. Therefore, the opening and closing price levels could be shown at the appropriate level as small branches coming out of the main bar. Closing prices are placed right at the bar. Prices for opening are on the left hand side.

How to Read Bar Charts

Bar charts consist of a foot opening, a vertical line and a foot closing. The bar contains the time-frame open, high, low, and near, as well as the direction (up or down) and time-frame range.

You can read the bar chart during live trading, like this:

1.) Open–The open is the first price exchanged at the bar and is marked on the left side of the bar by the horizontal foot.

2.) High–The highest price exchanged during the bar, and the top of the vertical bar is indicated.

3.) High–The lowest price exchanged at the bar is shown at the bottom of the vertical column.

4.) Close–The closing is the last price exchanged during the bar, and the horizontal foot on the right side of the bar is indicated.

5.) Position—The positions of the opening and closing feet show the position of the bar. The bar is an upward bar if the closing foot is above the opening foot, and if the closing foot is below the opening foot, then the bar is a downward bar. Sometimes you can paint these bars with a charting program, in which case the upward bars are usually colored white, and the downward bars are colored in red.

6.) Scope-The bar scope is defined by the top and bottom positions of the bottle. Calculating the range is by subtracting the low from the high (range= high-low).

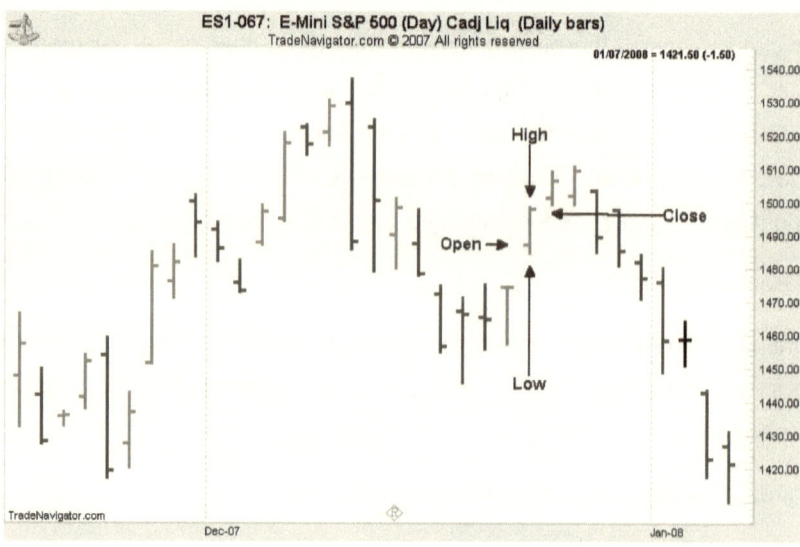

CANDLESTICK CHARTS

Candlestick charts are not recent-Japanese traders have used them to forecast and act on market movements for hundreds of years.

Charting of the candlesticks provides further insight into human psychology.

In the 1700's, Homma, a Japanese rice merchant, discovered how human psychology affected the price of rice as much as the supply and demand situation. Homma traded rice using candlestick charts and amassed a huge fortune in the markets. It was reportedly rumored he had never had a single losing trade!

Human psychology has never changed; it has remained constant over time–charting candlesticks is just as useful today as it was centuries ago. Even though they may look a little confusing, several fantastic reasons are available to use candlestick charts. Here are the most significant ones:

Complement Other Technical Tools

As you would use the modern bar chart, you can use candlestick charts and combine these with traditional market indicators. Candlestick charts are a great way to use other metrics to spot openings, screen, and time trades.

Spotting Pattern Shifts

Due to the way candlestick charts are presented, they can give you a much better visual warning of market reversals than conventional bar charts. When you look at the charting of the candlestick, the human psychology of the move practically leaps at you from the paper.

Using Conventional Bar Charts And Draw Them Quickly

The different names of candles are easy to remember, using chandelier charts straightforwardly using the same open, high, low and near data.

Defining Market Momentum

The way the candlestick chart is drawn provides not only the path-price, but also the energy behind the shift.

How to Read Candlestick Charts

Candlestick charts are a broad vertical line and a narrow vertical line. Each candlestick includes the timeframe open, high, low, and close-frame, timeframe direction (upward or downward), and timeframe range. You can read the candlestick chart during live trading as follows:

1.) Open–The open is the first price exchanged during the candlestick and is shown by either the top or bottom of the large vertical line (the bottom of the upward candlestick and the top of the downward candlestick).

2.) High –The highest price exchanged during the candle–stick, shown by the top of the thin vertical bar (candlestick wick).

3.) Low –The lowest price sold during the candlestick is shown by the bottom of the thin vertical bar (the candlestick's upside down wick).

4.) Close–The closing is the last price exchanged during the candlestick and is indicated either by the top or bottom of the long vertical line (the top of the candlestick upwards and the bottom of the candlestick downwards).

5.) Direction-The candlestick direction is indicated by the candlestick color (specifically the long vertical line). If the candlestick is usually green, the candlestick is an upward one and if the candlestick is red, the candlestick is a downward candlestick, but these colors can be personalized. The upward candlesticks are white in the map below, and the downward candlesticks are black in color.

6.) Range–The range of the candlestick is indicated by the locations of the top and bottom of the thin vertical lines (the wicks). Subtracting the low from the high (scale= high-low) determines the range.

The body of the candlestick chart graphically illustrates the relationship behind the open, high, low, and near, adding an extra visual edge because of the way they are depicted.

The candlestick has a large portion, called the "true body." This real body reflects the spectrum between that day's open and close trading.

If the actual body is packed with blood, the closure is lower than the open. If the real body is black, the opposite is said—the closure was higher than the open.

We see the "shadows" above and under the real body. We see these as the candle wicks (which give them their name). The shadows actually show the day trading high and low.

If the upper shadow on the filled-in red body is low, this means that the opening that day was closer to the day's peak. On the other hand, on a green or unfilled body, a short upper shadow shows the close has been near the high.

Whether you're a day trader, a position trader, a machine trader, or a trader who likes to do your own business, there's nothing to hate about candlestick charts, anyway.

They are easy to use, and are fun to use. In addition, they provide greater insight into market movements, as well as the flexibility to be used in any type of trade. If you're not already using charting candlesticks then it's time to start.

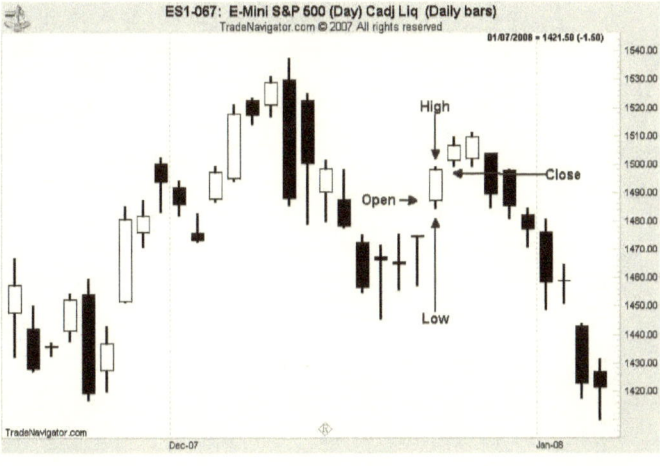

LINE CHARTS

A simple chart of lines draws a line between one closing price and the next closing price. Line charts show the general movement of prices over a period of time. Some investors and traders think closing is more relevant than open, high or low. You will overlook intraday fluctuations by paying attention to just the near.

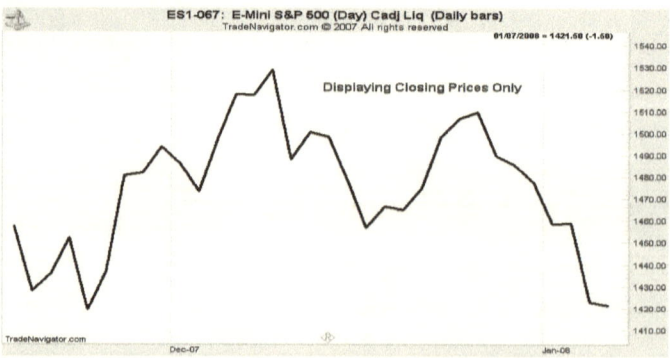

Line charts are also used when the data points are not available, high, and low. Sometimes for other indexes, thinly traded securities, and intraday prices, only the closing data are available.

How to Interpret Line Charts

Line charts are made of individual points attached to straight lines. That point usually indicates the timeline completion, but this can be changed to display either data – available, high or low. Line charts also show the direction of the timeframe (upwards or downwards).

Using Charts in Your Trading

Most charting software supports charts for bars, candlesticks and line. Normally, the show and the colors can be personalized according to your desire.

You can use any accurate charting tool you want online. Only insure that they provide the necessary analytical tools (e.g., the ability to draw trend lines, and the option to add moving averages). There are so many charting tools out there that in fact, it would be impossible to name some.

Just put it that way: charts are not the trading crystal ball.

Charts neither predict future consumer activities nor estimate market prices. They offer you a concise and precise history of a given market's price movements. There's a pattern in that past and it's from this background that you can extrapolate evidence on which to build your future projections on possible consumer trends and price changes. That is the greatest value you will get when using maps.

TECHNICAL INDICATORS

Let's keep it simple: if you buy when the market is up and sell when the market is down, you'll make money. That's why technical analysts are holding to the motto "the trend is your friend." Finding the prevailing trend in the market will help you become aware of the overall direction of the market and give you better visibility—especially when short-term movements tend to clutter the image.

TRENDS

A security price chart may seem like a random distribution, but this is not so.

Approximately 30 per cent of the time, there will be a definite trend in security. The rest of the time, stocks are more or less likely to be traded sideways. Our task is to detect trends early when they emerge out of non-trends, or as reversals of previous trends.

Our aim is to buy or sell our security early on in these new trends, thus profitably exiting trade when the trend ends. The most critical role we have as traders is to recognize the pattern, both its beginning and end.

A basic trend description is, in essence, the general direction of price movements. If markets make a series of higher highs and higher lows, there is an uptrend. There is a downward trend as prices make a number of lower and lower highs.

Prices are said to be moving sideways in a sequence, or trendless trading, when prices move without such a discernible pattern. Once a trend is discernible, trend lines can then be drawn to describe a downtrend's lower limits or upper limits.

It is important that the trend lines are correctly drawn. It is trend line identification and the breach of this trend line that is the key to successful trading and building wealth.

Does it all sound too simple?

I know those basic concepts sound boring, and many traders want to jump right into complex metrics and complicated trading strategies. Make no mistake of that.

Trading can be simple: you buy when the market is going up and you sell when the market is going down. That's how they make money.

But if you don't know how to identify when the market is through and when it's going down, then you're going to lose money really quickly. So you MUST find a clear way to identify business direction.

The easiest way of doing that is to use trend lines.

Indicators are another way to determine market direction, but if you know how to use clear trend lines to define the trend, then you will never have to think about indicators again.

The only two remaining questions are:*

- **When should I sign in?**
- **When do I need to exit?**

Just keep reading for the answers.

Uptrend

Let me show you exactly how to draw a trend line.

The accompanying diagram is an E-mini S&P5-minute bar chart. Trading day is December 20, 2007

As you can see, prices went down all morning, and then they started moving sideways during the break at lunch. We see the low of the day at 11:50pm (Central Standard Time)

Prices find resistance at 1462.50, and at 12:25pm high volume prices break resistance. Prices are clearly on the upward track now, and it is time to draw our trend line.

Trend lines are drawn below prices in an uptrend, while trend lines are drawn above prices in a downtrend. We need two points, in order to draw a line. The first point is the day's low and the second point is the first retraction as rates do not make higher lows any longer.

90

At 12:15pm bar, the first time prices do not make a higher low happens, and we can draw our trendline. The dark portion of the line is the confirmed trend, and the projected trend is the light part of the line.

At 12:35pm we see for the second time a lower low in an upward trend, but we do NOT change the trendline. In general, trendlines can only get flatter, not steeper. Adjusting the trendline to the second low would create a steeper trendline, so no change is made.

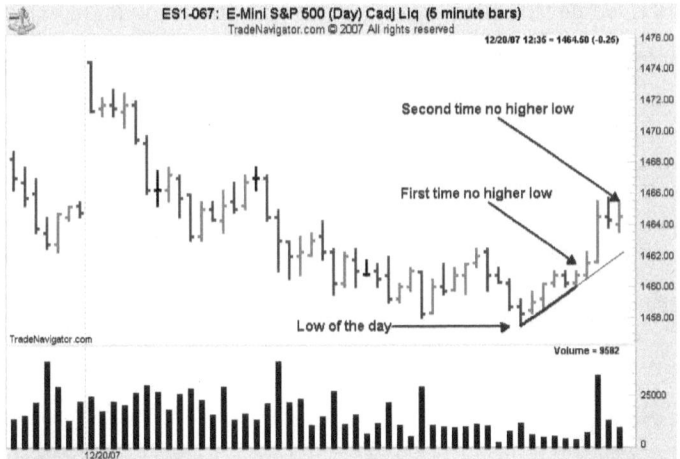

A lower low is made again at 12:45pm and 12:50pm, and this time we will change the trend line. It's just a slight adjustment and the trend line is - it's going a bit flatter. All previous prices are above the trend line, therefore the trend remains intact. The next low occurs at 1:05pm, and we can stretch our trendline. It's a simple extension: no change is required, and we see that the uptrend has been in place for 40 minutes, since the breakout at 12:25pm at 1462.50 through the resistance level.

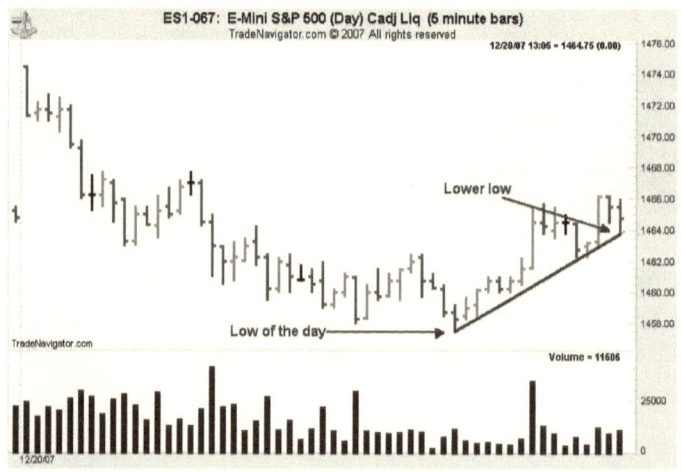

Ten minutes later, we get the next lower low, and the trend line is adjusted accordingly. See how pretty the lower preceding lows almost hit the trend line? A pattern to perfection.

We see a lower low again but we don't change the trend line because it would make the line steeper. Remember the rule: we can just flatten the line, we can't steeper it up.

Another low occurs at 1:50pm but the trend line is not changed.

We see a number of lower lows in this next chart but only the lower at 2:05pm helps us to change the trend line. The sequence of lows below indicates the phenomenon is coming to an end.

Fifteen minutes later, we have another lower low but at the same time, after a sequence of lower heights, we are reaching a higher height. Lower highs suggest a potential downtrend, and it's time to start drawing a downtrend line when we see the first higher up.

Our uptrend is quickly coming to an end. The line of uptrend is broken, and we have another higher high which confirms our line of downtrend.

The uptrend was in effect for a full two hours, from 12:25pm until 2:25pm. During this time, prices rose to a peak of 1472 from 1462.50 (a break through resistance level). At 1467.75 the uptrend broke.

There are two important things to remember about trend lines: Never adjust a trend line so it gets steeper. Don't use price bars to run a trend line. There is always an uptrend line under the price bars.

Hold a trendline near the lower lows and don't push it too far.

If your line is too far from the lower lows, you risk missing a pattern shift.

Downtrend

In a similar way to the uptrend line, a downtrend line is built. The main difference is that you are aiming for a higher high and you are drawing the price bars on the trend line ABOVE.

Here we've got an E-mini S&P5-minute chart on December 20, 2007. The opening price is also the highest price, and we have the first higher, at 8:45am, 15 minutes after the opening. So we can draw our line on the downtrend.

The market is continuing to fall and we see the next higher peak at 9:10am. We don't change the trend line, though, since that would mean steepening the line.

We see another higher high at 9:35am but the trend line is still not changed. The bar of 9:40am marks yet another high and supports our previous trend line.

Ten minutes and two bars later, we've got another higher, and we're able to adjust our thread. Remember that it is still very similar to the previous highs, so the setting is correct.

The market is making another higher level, but we are not changing the trend line because it would make the line steeper. See how beautiful the downtrend is captured by our trend line?

The trend continues, and we can adjust the trend line again at 11:15am, almost three hours after the opening. The trend line is still very close to the higher elevations above.

Fifteen minutes later, we get the next higher, but if we change the trend line, it's going to move it too far from the previous higher elevations; the downtrend is broken

Adjusting the trend line will push it too far from previous highs and we risk missing a trend shift.

Trend line Validity

A trend line's validity depends on its length, and how many times it has been successfully tested. The longer the trend line has been in place, and the more successfully it has been checked, the stronger the trend line is. Consequently, when a long-term trend line—which has been successfully tested many times—is violated, there is likely to have been a significant reversal of the trend.

Trend lines and Trend Channels

Trend lines are basic but helpful instruments to confirm market trends direction. A straight line ascending is formed by joining at least two consecutive lows. The second point must of course be higher than the first.

The line's continuation helps determine the direction the market is going along. A trend upward is a clear way of identifying sup-port lines / levels. By contrast, downward lines are charted by connecting two or more points. A trading line's validity is correlated in part with the number of connection points. It is worth mentioning, however, that points should not be too close to each other.

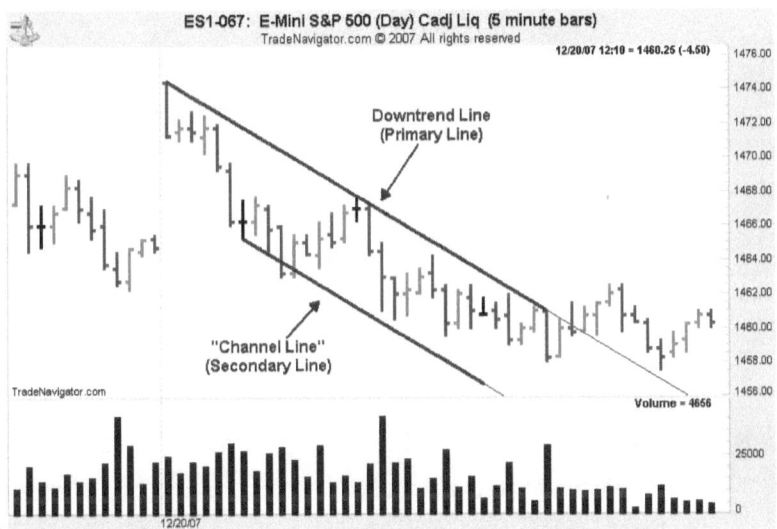

A channel is characterized by two parallel trend lines as the price direction drawn. For the size, the lines serve as up, down, or straight corridor. Remember that you first draw the trend line when drawing trend channels, and then create the "channel line" as a parallel line to the primary trend line. Typically trend channels are constructed in an uptrend or downtrend to derive entry and exit points.

In a downtrend, as shown in the following example, you will sell on the primary downtrend line and buy back on the secondary channel line.

POPULAR TRADING APPROACHES

You know by now, every sector is either a trendy or a moving side-ways. So you're going to apply one of the following two trading strategies:

1.) Trend-following: When prices go up, you buy and when prices go down, you sell.

101

2.) Trend-fading: When prices are moving to the extreme (e.g. upper channel band), you sell, and then you try to catch a small move when prices are reverting to "normality."

Most of the indicators you will find in your charting software belong to one of these two categories: trend-identification indicators (e.g. moving averages) or indicators that identify over-bought or over-sold situations that provide you with a short-term swinging trading setup.

Don't get confused about all the possibilities of entering into a deal. Just make sure you understand the reason you're using a given indicator and the indicator measurement.

Here are a few examples of common trading approaches: Trend-following: Moving Averages Crossover of Moving Averages Turtle Trading Average Convergence-Divergence (MACD) Trend-fading: Williams percent R Relative Strength Index (RSI) Bollinger Bands and ChannelsBollinger Bands and Channels

SIMPLE MOVING AVERAGES

If you believe in the technical analysis tenet "trend-is-your-friend," moving averages (MA) are of great help. Moving averages tell the aver-age price in a given point of time over a defined period of time, typically the closing price. These are named' running' as these mimic the current average when adhering to the same amount of time.

A weakness of moving averages is that they lag the market, so they do not necessarily signal a change in trends. To address this issue, use a shorter period, such as a 5-or 10-day moving average, that is more representative of the recent price action than the moving averages of 40 or 200 days. The concept is simple: when the closing price moves above the moving average, a buy signal is produced.

When the closing price drops below the moving average, a selling signal is produced. Here is an example using Amazon's 10-minute map (AMZN).

You can see that this strategy works very well in trend markets (see first buy signal), but you get whip-sawed (see second buy signal) in laterally shifting markets.

The Right Concept for the Right Market

A lot of traders every day seek to use strategies that are based on moving averages. And then they lament that those strategies are not working.

Keep in mind that this is a trend-following approach–it should be extended only to the fashionable markets.

You might want to use trendlines or other measures to make sure the market you are monitoring is trending, and then use moving aver-ages to get your precise signals for entry.

Crossover of Moving Averages

The use of two moving averages is another very popular approach: a "fast" moving average (e.g. 14 bars) and a "slow" moving average (e.g. 20 bars). The number of days used for the slow-moving average has to be greater than the number of days used for the fast-moving average.

When the rapidly moving average crosses the slow moving average from below a buy signal is generated.

When the fast-moving average crosses the slow moving average from above a sell signal is produced.

Here is one example from this strategy:

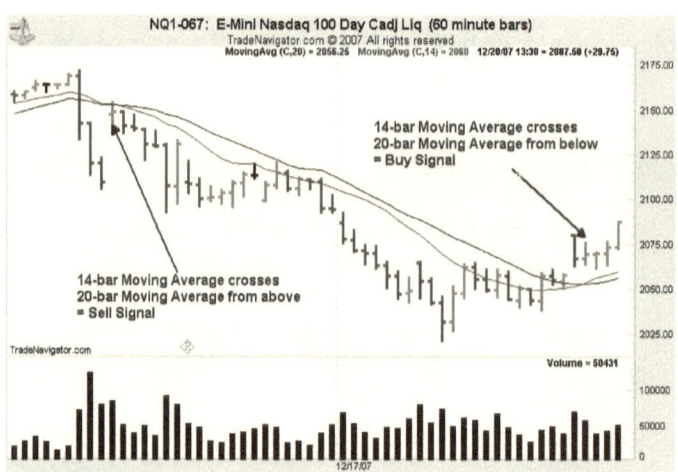

The upper line is the average slow moving (20 bars), and the lower line is the average fast moving (14 bars).

TURTLE TRADING

On the Internet, you will find plenty of articles that will explain in detail the rules of the turtle trade. Basically, through the past 20 days, the turtles look at the high and the low, and generate the following signals:

When the current prices move higher than the previous 20 bars, a buy signal is generated.

A selling signal is generated when current prices move below the preceding 20 bar low.

Prices moved below the low of 20 bar at 1,4372 and a short signal was produced. Prior to retracing, rates fell as low as 1.4324 (= 48 pips or 480).

We just identified an entry signal, please note.

Moving Average Convergence Divergence (MACD)

104

The Moving Average Convergence / Divergence (MACD), created by Gerald Apple, is another trend-following predictor. This indicator shows the relation between two moving price averages. For the MACD, the most common parameter is the difference between an exponential moving average (EMA) of 26 bar and the 12 bar. It then plots this difference on the chart and oscillates above and below zero.

The MACD's 9-bar EMA, called the "signal line," is then plotted on top of the MACD, which functions as a buy and sell signal trigger (dark gray line).

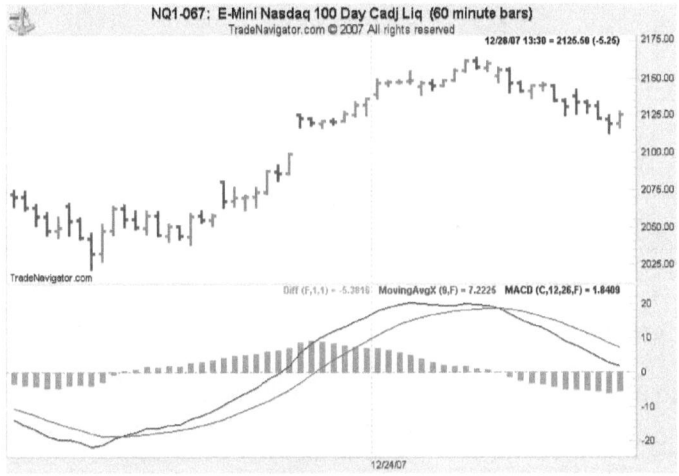

Traders use the MACD in various ways, but the most popular is to use the signal line for input signals: when the signal line (dark grey line) crosses the MACD (light grey line) from below, a buy signal is generated.

When the signal line (dark grey line) crosses the MACD (light grey line) from above, a sell signal is generated.

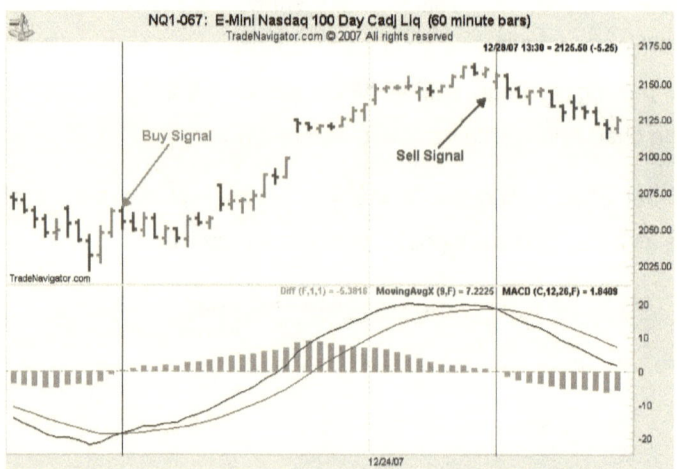

Williams %R

Williams percent R is one of the most common overbought / sold indicators.

This metric was created by Larry Williams in 1966 to help the traders distinguish market positions that are overbought and oversold.

Williams percent R, also referred to as percent R, over a certain period of time compared a stock close to the high-low range.

The calculation is quite simple: it subtracts the close of the current day from the lowest intraday low of the last number of days of' X' and then divides this difference by the highest minus the lowest of the last number of days of' X.' This calculation informs us where to the closing day is placed within the next day's range. If it is high in the range, the percentiles will be high, perhaps more than 80 percent. If we close low within the range of the last' X' number of days, that would be in the 20 percent or lower range.

106

The index has many applications, but the simplest one enables it to simply definitely or suggest an overbought, over-sold location.

The index can be used in any business and time frame. It is successfully used by most traders on intraday bar charts with a 14 bar parameter.

The indicator shows the closing price relationship to a high-low range over a specific period of time, usually 14 bars, as mentioned above.

The outcome is plotted on a map, and ranges from 0 to 100. The basic idea is that if prices are trading at the high of the high-low range (indicator reading nearly 100), then the market is overbought, and if current prices are trading near the low of the specified range (indicator reading close to 0), then the market is over-sold.

When the indicator has a value above 80 a sell signal is produced.

When the indicator has a value below 20 a buy signal is produced.

The percentage R moves above 80 in this example chart, indicating that Google (GOOG) is "over-sold," and generating a selling signal.

Williams per cent R works best in lateral markets.

RELATIVE STRENGTH INDEX (RSI)

The Relative Strength Index (RSI), developed by Welles Wilder, is another popular overbought / oversold indicator. The RSI compares the magnitude of the recent gains of a stock to the magnitude of its recent losses and turns it into a number ranging from 0 to 100. It takes one parameter to use in the calculation of the number of time periods. Wilder recommends using 14 time periods in his book.

When the RSI traverses the 70-line (over -bought-zone) from above, a sell signal is generated.

When the RSI crosses the 30-line (over -sold-zone) from below a buy signal is generated.

The RSI dips below 30 and produces a buy signal, coincidentally at day's bottom. Profits could be realized very rapidly by implementing stop loss and benefit exit strategies (see next chapter).

The RSI measure works best in laterally moving stocks, as with the percent R.

BOLLINGER BANDS AND CHANNELS

Most traders are familiar with the "Bollinger Bands" concept. Bollinger Bands consist of a moving average and two regular deviations, one above and one below the moving average. The main thing to learn about Bollinger Bands is that, depending on the settings, they contain up to 95 per cent of closing price.

The most common setting for the upper and lower bands is a 21 bar moving average (solid dark grey line) and 2 standard deviations (pointed grey line).

When prices move beneath the lower Bollinger Band, a buy signal is generated.

When prices move above the upper Bollinger Band a sell signal is produced.

This is an E-mini S&P10-minute view. After morning's sluggish trading, prices move beyond the upper Bollinger Band and produce a sell signal.

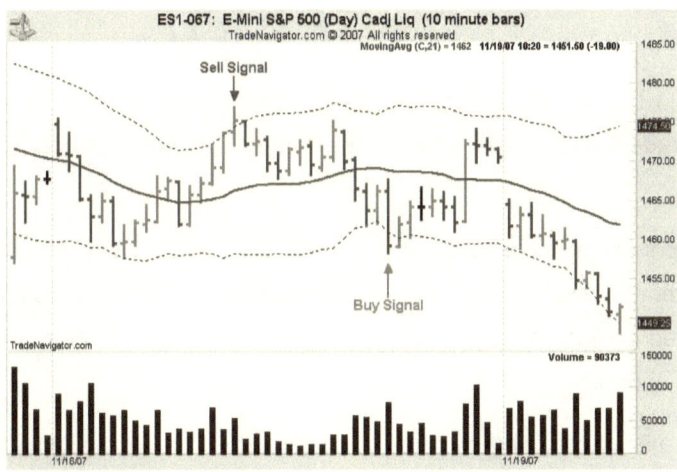

Two hours later, prices move below the lower Bollinger Band and a buy signal is created.

This indicator works best in markets which are moving sideways.

Trading Approaches

Before deciding on a trading approach, you need to identify whether the market is trending or moving sideways.

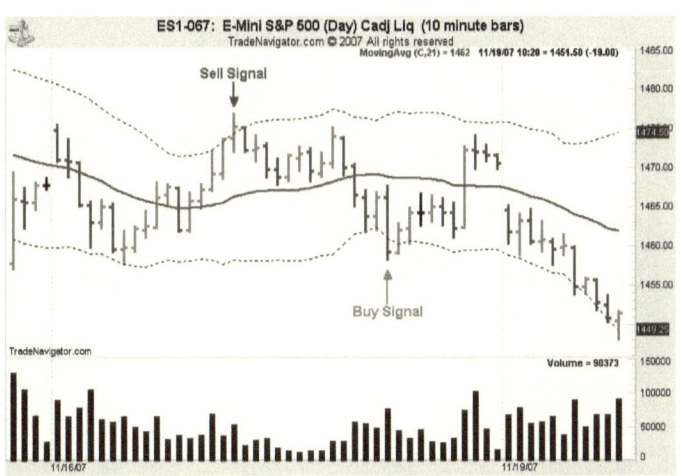

Don't fall prey to the common mistakes. Many traders simply decide on one trading approach and trade it all the time, whether the market is trending or not. That's a sure way to failure.

Successful traders use multiple trading approaches: they have at least one approach for a trending market and another approach for a sideways-moving market. Using the basic principles outlined on page 103, you can determine the direction of the market and use the right trading approach.

Don't make the mistake of using only **one** trading approach. Learn to identify whether a market is trending or not and adjust your trading strategy accordingly.

TRADING RANGE

This is a pattern of exchange that exists between uptrend and downtrend-trend. This refers to an offers and demand equilibrium. Trends at the sideways follow a horizontal direction, where the price remains relatively constant. Trading patterns are also used to set levels of support and resistance which are very useful for charts technical analysis.

Defining Entry Points

As you saw in the examples above, most of the trading approaches or indicators already provide you with rules of entry. You want to keep it clear and precise when identifying entry points. The economy is not freezable. A market is constantly on the move, and you need to make your trade decisions quickly.

Many trading strategies and metrics include a bar end judgment. Even when you're watching 60 minute bars, and you've spent the past hour doing nothing but waiting for your cue, now—at the end of the bar—you've just got a split second to decide.

Use as few rules of entry as possible, and be as specific as possible. The best trading strategies have rules of entry which you can define in just two lines.

Defining Exit Points

This chapter is probably the most significant chapter in the whole book. I once heard the saying, "A monkey can go into a trade, but when you exit it, money is made (and lost). Most traders are right when entering a trade about the direction of the market, but they end up losing because they fail to capture profits at the right time.

Read this chapter over and over until you get ALL of the concepts outlined here. It will ultimately determine your success or failure as a trader to know HOW and WHEN to exit a trade.

You should apply three different exit rules: Stop the rules on losses to protect your capital. Taking advantage of exits to make your gains come true. If the market is not moving at all, time-stops to get you out of a trade and free your capital stop loss and profit-taking exit rules can be expressed in four ways: A fixed dollar amount (e.g. $1,000) A percentage of the current price (e.g. 1 percent of the entry price) A percentage of volatility (e.g. 50 percent of the average daily move) Based on technical analysis (e.g. support and resistance levels) These exit strategies will be discussed in detail in the following.

Stop Losses

A stop loss is used if the trade goes against you to limit the potential loss. It's the point to which you're going to close a trade on the grounds that it's gone too far in the' wrong' direction, thereby negating the reason you're in that company.

Always use losses on stops!

If you don't apply stop losses in your trading, you're not going to trad for long–you're going to end up wiping your trading balance out in no time. It can be too simple for a loss of $300 to become a loss of $5,000. A successful trader is going to know when to take a small loss and go on to the next contract.

I can't stress this enough: even the most experienced traders, whether they are trading forex, futures, options or even stocks, have a stop loss order on the market. Remember your trading capital is your business-there is no insurance if you burn it. You're done. Once you've entered a deal, you'll be putting a stop immediately. Which keeps you from losing all of your money?

Don't Forget Your Stop Losses!

When you close your place, it's important to make sure your stop is cancelled. I mention this because I know a very disciplined trader who always gets into a stop loss and a profit target order once a trade has been formed. Over the course of several days this trader incurred a number of losses a few years back. And, of course, he was quite pleased to see a trade going in his direction at last.

His stop losses were very low, according to his plan, and his profit goal was rather high, so if this trade met the profit target, he would compensate for all the losses of the past couple of days PLUS would bring a small profit on top of it.

And it happened: the market kept moving in his favor, then he finally — made a profit.

He was so excited he leapt out of his chair, raced into the kitchen and told his wife everything about the great deal. He made some money in FINALLY. Together, they shared a nice cup of coffee and he couldn't stop talking about his plan, the trade and how it paid off.

And when a hour later he returned to his computer he found himself in a position of failure.

He was unable to believe it! Why did it happen?

It dawned on him after a few minutes: he had forgotten to cancel his loss of the stop. When celebrating his victory, the market retraced and filled out his order, and then went up again.

The order to stop loss was a sell order, and in a rising market the trader now had a short position. All its revenues have gone.

Story morale: make sure your orders are canceled, or use so-called "bracket orders," or "one-cancel-other (OCO) orders" for your benefit target and avoid loss. These words can be explained to you in depth by your broker.

The most important thing, no matter how you approach the decision, is to know where you will be cutting a losing position before you enter the trade. Set the rules, and follow them always. With that in mind, let's talk about strategies to stop loss.

Fixed Dollar Amount

Simple, simple and straight forward. Simply determine a dollar amount you're willing to risk, delete it from your entry price, and place an order for stop loss.

How to use this strategy: just subtract from your entry price the dollar amount you specified.

Example: Suppose you are trading the currency pair EUR / USD. At 1.4585, you've entered the market and you want to gamble $100. Because 1 pip (= 0.0001) is equal to $10, at 1.4575, you put your stop loss at 10 pips (= 0.0010) below your entry price.

Just as a reminder:

If you're a security guy for a long time, you'll sell it to close the place. If a security is short you must buy it to close the place. I know that sounds stupid, but you wouldn't believe how many traders get con-fused; they'll add to their spot instead of closing.

When the market starts moving fast and you get anxious, it is easy to make mistakes. Most traders use post-its after entering a trade: if you've gone long, you put a' SELL' post-it on your phone, and a' BUY' post-it if you've gone far. This way you make sure you exit the role as expected always

When to Use This Strategy:

This strategy is ideal for beginners, since complex calculations are not necessary. You either add or subtract the lack of stop to or from your entry price and that's it. It works best if you transact just one stock or one sector, and if there is not too much fluctuation in price.

How to Use This Strategy:

To get your exit point, simply multiply the entry price by (1-your stop loss (in percentage form)) when you apply this stop loss strategy.

Example: If you're trading the E-mini NASDAQ and you've defined a stop loss of 0.5 percent, you'd multiply your entry price by 0.995 (1-0.5 percent) for a 2141 exit point.

When to Use This Strategy:

If you trade multiple markets or specific stocks, you can apply this exit strategy. The next segment includes a more detailed explanation: "Profit-Taking Exits."

Percentage of the Volatility

This exit strategy is another way for the volatile markets to specify stop losses. The underlying idea is to change the stop loss based on market volatility: you are applying a greater stop loss in volatile markets as well as a smaller stop loss in quiet markets.

How to Use This Strategy:

Using this benefit exit strategy would entail two steps: First, you must assess a market's average volatility. Second, multiply the number by the specified percentage.

Using Technical Analysis

To order to determine their exits, many traders like to use major support or resistance points on the map. You could use Pivot Points, Fibonacci Levels, upper or lower trend channel levels, or Bollinger Bands instead of help and resistance levels, just to name a few.

How to Use This Strategy:

Simply use technical analysis to identify a potential loss of the stop.

Example: In this example, to determine our stop loss we use a simple trend line. The accompanying diagram is an Apple Computer (AAPL) 15 minute map. We are waiting for the first bar of the day and we sell short at $184.80 as soon as we know the stock moves down over the first 15 minutes. We're drawing a trend line from the top of the previous day to the top of the bar this morning and setting our stop loss at $187.50.

When to Use This Strategy:

This strategy is perfect for traders who use technical analysis for their entry points. If you're using trend lines, indicators, or support and resistance lines, placing your stop at these levels will seem very natural.

Profit-Taking Exits

Once you're in a profitable trade, when to take the benefit becomes the next challenge.

The main problem with profit taking is that we humans (and particularly traders) are greedy by our very nature. We want to make money, after all. Much capital. and let's make it quick. "Hurry to get rich," right?

That's a definite problem and a lot of traders are too selfish. We just want to become rich on one trade. And that is when they are struggling.

Here's the key to successful trading: reliably, modest gains.

Consistency is the key, because if your profits are consistent and predict-capable then you can just use leverage to size the trade. So you MUST know when to exit on a score.

Better traders make use of a stop loss; big traders use a profit target.

Here are various forms of exit strategies for profitable trades.

Fixed Dollar Amount

This is the easiest way of exiting a company. Simply define a dollar amount you'd be satisfied with, add it to your entry point and market a benefit goal order.

How to Use This Strategy: Simply add to your entry price the dollar amount that you mentioned.

Example: Let's assume you transact 100 IBM shares and join at $110.13. Your profit target is $100, so as soon as prices go up $1 to $111.13 you'd exit the deal.

When to use this strategy: This strategy works better if you are merely trading one stock or one market, and if there is not too much fluctuation in the stability.

Percentage of the current price

How to use this strategy: Simply multiply the entry price by (1+ your profit target (in percent)) to get your exit point when you apply this profit exit strategy.

Example: If you're trading IBM, and you've set a 1 percent profit target, you'd multiply your $110.13 entry price by 1.01 (1 + 1 percent) for a $111.23 exit point.

When to use this approach: When you trade multiple markets or specific stocks, you can apply this exit strategy.

The reason is simple: let's assume that you trade IBM and Ford. IBM selling at $110.13 as I write this, and Ford trading at $6.72 as well. Let's assume, as in the previous example, that you trade 100 shares each and that you want to make $100 per trade. IBM would only have to move 0.9 percent to reach your profit target, but to reach your profit target, Ford shares would have to move nearly 15 per cent.

Specifying the profit target as a percentage of the price would make more sense-e.g. 1 per cent. In this scenario, to get to the profit goal, IBM would have to move $1.1 and Ford just $0.07.

The same applies to high volatility markets, such as gold futures or oil futures. Gold was trading at $650, at the beginning of 2007. Gold turnover was 30 per cent higher in November 2007, at $850. In January 2007, a $20 change in gold would have been 3 per cent, but only 2.3 per cent in November 2007.

Percentage of the Volatility

This exit strategy is another way for the volatile markets to identify income goals. The underlying idea is to change your profit target based on market volatility: you apply a higher profit goal in volatile markets and a lower profit goal in quiet markets.

How to Use This Strategy: Using this strategy of exiting income needs two steps:

First, you calculate the average market price.

Second, multiply the number by the specified percentage.

For an example see the comments in the "Avoid Losses" section.

When to Use This Strategy: This strategy is suitable for commodity markets with high volatility shifts, such as the grain and energy markets.

Using Technical Analysis Most traders like to assess their exits using major support or resistance points on the board. You could use Pivot Points, Fibonacci Levels, Upper or Lower trend channel levels, or Bollinger Bands instead of support and resistance levels, just to name a few.

How to Use This Strategy: Use the Technical Analytics process to identify a potential profit target.

118

Example: We use high and low of the previous day as potential profit targets in this example. The following chart is an E-mini S&P 15 minute chart. We are waiting for the first bar of the day, and as soon as we realize that the market has moved up in the first 15 minutes, we enter at 1452.

We have set our profit target to the high of the previous day–1465.25–for a total profit of 13.25 points= $662.50. We reached our profit tar later that day-get, and we were able to reverse the position by going short. We can now use the previous day low as a profit target and realize another 21.75 point profit= $1,087.50.

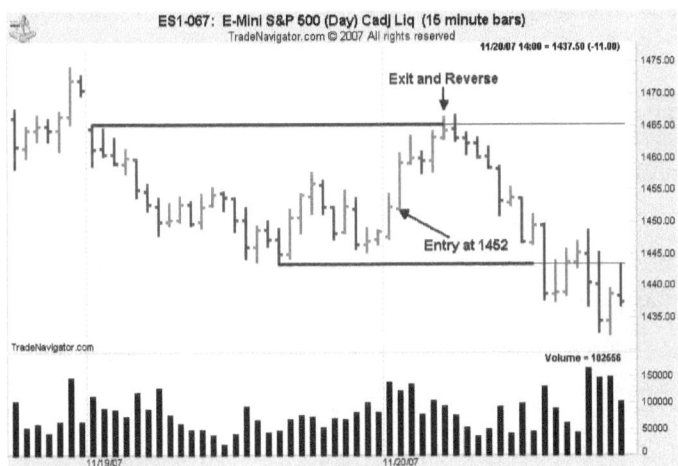

When to use this strategy: This strategy is ideal for markets that switch sideways between major support lines and lines of resistance.

Trailing stops

Trailing stops are stops which are "hybrid." The trailing stop is usually a stop loss when entering a position, and as the trade moves in your favor, the trailing stop becomes a benefit exit.

The main difference between the above exit strategies and trailing stops is that you change your stop continuously while you're in a deal. All other exit strategies are "set-it - and-forget-it-strategies," in which you define stop loss and exit points as soon as you enter the trade, and then leave them alone until you close the business.

How to Use This Strategy: This strategy can be used in tandem with place-by-place technical analysis-the stop at lines of support and resistance or, more precisely, the high or low previous floor. Another popular use of this strategy is to place the stops on trend-following indicators such as Moving Averages or Parabolic. Most traders tend to use a set amount of the dollar.

Example 1: Fixed Dollar Amount:

If you set a straight $300 trailing stop, and the security moved by $1,000 to your advantage, you could change your stop to just $300 behind the price and lock in $700 of profit.

Example 2: Technical Analysis:

Below is an E-mini S&P 60-minute table. Let's assume that at 1502, you went short. At 1504, you would put your trailing stop at the top of the current bar. Upon completion of the next bar, you move your stop to the top of this bar to 1502.50 You switch your stop to 1499 60 minutes later, and now your lack of stoppage becomes a benefit exit. Whatever happens with the trade now, you are going to earn at least 3 points (= $150). You switch your stop one hour later to 1494.50

So you're stopped at 1494.50 for a benefit of 7.5 points (= $375) when rates retrace.

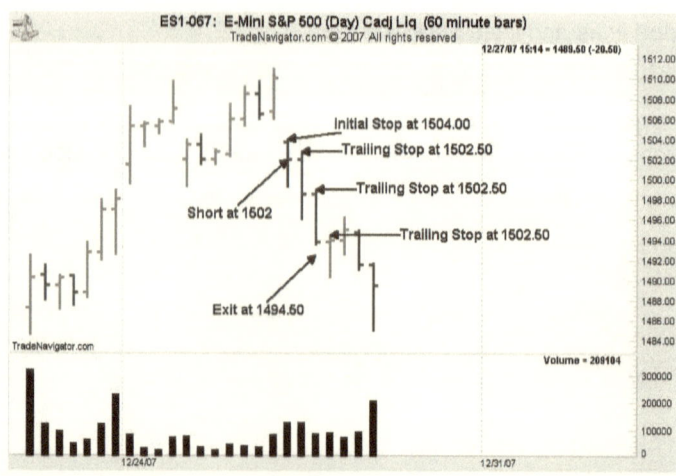

When to Use This Strategy: Ideal for trend markets. For take advantage of longer-lasting patterns, you should use that technique. Keep in mind that this strategy requires your constant attention because according to your rules, you Will shift your trailing stops.

Taking Partial Profits

No one ever lost money.

For more sophisticated exit strategies you can combine the strategies outlined above. As an example, once you've earned a set dollar amount of earnings, you might close half of your position, and let the other half continue to trade to the next level of support or resistance.

Or you could take 1/3 of your profits to a predefined profit goal, take another 1/3 of your profits to the next level of support and resistance, and add a trail-stop to the remaining 1/3.

The possibilities are endless. That's why a lot of professional traders are trying to improve their exit strategy. Most novice traders and beginners, by comparison, tend to focus on entry strategies.

Don't make exactly the same mistake. Once you have established rules for sound entry check through exit strategies to maximize your income.

Time-Stops

A time-stop will get you out of a trade unless it goes in any direction at all. You have probably a good reason to enter a trade. So, you submit your stop loss and your income goal immediately after entering, and wait. And just wait. And just wait. And it doesn't happen.

Close to escape. When markets are not going anyway, get out.

How to Use This Strategy: Simply define a "time-out," after which the business will be exit. Then set a timer and exit the trade after the specified time irrespective of whether you have met your stop loss or benefit objective.

Example: Three times the timeframe you are using is a good time-stop. If you use 15-minute maps, you might want to abandon the trade if after 45 minutes you don't hit either your benefit or your stop loss. If you use charts for 60 minutes, get out after 3 hours.

When to put this technique to use: Sometimes! Whatever the reason behind your signal to join, you want to see something happening. If after a certain amount of time nothing occurs, the underlying assumption about your entry may be false. If you're staying in the business then you're not trading gambling.

As traders, we want to make quick money. The longer you're in the market with your money, the longer it's at risk. Through implementing a time-stop and leaving the market, you will significantly reduce the risk when it does not shift. Free your money and take the next opportunity to trade. Don't play!

Step 6: Evaluating Your Strategy

It's time to test and evaluate your trading strategy once you've determined which markets you want to trade, se-leased a timeframe, and defined your entry and exit rules.

There are three ways to test your trading strategy:

Back-Testing

Back-Testing is a test method that will run your strategy against periods of prior time. Basically, you're doing a simulation: you're using your strategy to test its effectiveness with relevant past data. You're saving a ton of time by using the historical data; if you've tried to test your plan by applying it to the days yet to come, it could take you years. Back-testing is used for a variety of strategies, including technically analyzed ones. Back-testing reliability is based on the theory that what happened in the past will happen again in future. However, bear in mind that the effects of your back-testing are quite dependent on the moves that happened during the time period being tested. It's important to remember this in-creates risk potential for your strategy.

The Monte-Carlo Simulation

The Monte-Carlo Simulation is a problem-solving method used by running several experimental tests-called simulations-using random combinations to estimate the likelihood of certain outcomes. It is a way of accounting for the randomness of a parameter trading, usually the sequence of trades. The basic idea in Monte Carlo simulations is to take a sequence of trades created by a trading system, randomize the order of trades, and calculate the rate of return and the maximum drawdown, assuming that x% of the account is risked on each trading.

The process is repeated several hundred times, using a different random sequence of the same operations each time. You can then ask a question like "If 5% of the account is risky for each transaction, what is the probability that the maximum drawdown will be less than 25%?" If, for example, 1,000 random sequences of trades are simulated with 5% risk and 940 of them have a maximum drawdown of less than 25%, then you could say the likelihood of a maximum drawdown of less than 25%

Keep in mind that the data used in Monte Carlo Simulations are still historical data; thus, one might assume that this simulation is a more sophisticated back-testing process.

Paper Trading

Trading is a "risk-free" business practice. Basically, you set up a dummy account that allows you to test your business with paper money strategy. There are two ways to do this: either you can pretend to buy and sell stocks, bonds, commodities, etc., and keep track of your profits and losses on paper, or you can open an online account, usually through your broker (and usually free).

This is a great way of killing a whole tree full of birds with one stone for new traders. First off, you'll learn the tricks of trade without jeopardizing your own money. Second, when it comes to market maneuvering, you'll be able to earn some much-needed confidence. And thirdly, in real-time simulation, you'll be able to test your trade plan.

This is probably the best way to check a trade policy, because it is not based on historical evidence. On the other hand, it is the most time-consuming technique, as it may take weeks or months until you have enough data for a performance report that is statistically significant.

How long should you back-test a trading strategy?

The more trades you use in your back-testing, the higher the probability that your trading strategy will succeed in the future. Look at the following table:

Further trades mean a smaller margin of error, which results in a greater predictability of future performance.

Someone with a Ph.D. in statistics once told me you need at least 40 trades to produce results that are statistically significant.

So, the question "How long are you supposed to test your trade strategy?" Depends on level of exchange.

Improving Your Strategy

A device is differentiated between "improving" and "curve-fitting." Checking different exit methods will enhance the program. Use a trailing stop instead, if you are using a fixed stop.

Attach a time-stop, and reassess the results.

Look at the net income not only; look at the benefit factor, the average age profit per transaction, and the overall drawdown. Sometimes you'll see that when you add various stops the net profit marginally falls, but the other figures will improve dramatically. Don't fall into the trap of over-optimizing: by adding enough rules you can remove almost all losers, but your resulting plan will be virtually worthless.

CHAPTER 5: SUPPORT AND RESISTANCE

Levels of support and resistance are places where a map experiences recurrence-ringing pressure upwards or downwards. A level of support is usually the low point of any chart pattern (hourly, monthly, or annually), whereas a level of resistance is the maximum or highest point of the trend.

Such points are known as they display a propensity to reappear as support and resistance. Buying near support or selling near resistance levels is best, which are unlikely to be broken. Once they have reached those rates, they inevitably reverse their positions. Previous support transforms into opposition and previous resistance becomes support.

Levels of support and resistance are very important for your business; it's crucial you understand them.

During uptrends, whenever the price drops to the uptrend line, and then re-sums up its progress, the trend line has acted as support for the uptrend during price. Help can also be based on previous help or resistance rates.

During downtrends, the downtrend line has served as a barrier to the up-ward shift of market prices every time the price rises to the downtrend line and then resumes its decline.

Consider the following: the bulls (the buyers) take control when price action declines to a certain point and avoid prices from dropping below. Compared to help, a level of resistance is the point at which bears take control of prices (the sellers) and prevent them from rising higher.

The price a trade takes place at is the price a bull and bear decide to do business at. It represents their expectations on consensus. The bulls think prices are going to move higher and the bears think that prices are going to go down.

Support levels indicate the price at which a majority of investors think prices will rise upwards, and resistance levels indicate the price at which a majority of investors fear prices will move downwards.

The most visible and repeated occurrence on price charts is possibly the creation of support and resistance rates.

Example: Prices were in a downtrend as you can see from the following chart. Prices went to the resistance level at 1464.00 and retraced on the same bar that broke the downtrend. 10 Minutes later they went 2 ticks above the level of resistance, but closed AT the level of resistance.

Prices never go above the level of resistance of 1464 for the next 2 hours and 30 minutes, but they test this level repeatedly, and eventually break out.

If you draw a line of resistance, you will typically draw a corresponding line of support, as shown in the chart below.

As you can see, even though it is split later the support line holds very well. The break is not important, however, because prices close above the support line.

A Little More on Support and Resistance

Support is the level of price at which demand is considered to be strong enough to keep the price from further decreasing.

The logic dictates that as the price falls to help and becomes cheaper, buyers are more inclined to buy and sellers are less inclined to sell. It is believed that by the time the price reaches the level of support, demand will overcome supply and prevent the price from falling below support.

Resistance is the price level at which selling is considered to be strong enough to prevent further price increases.

The logic dictates that sellers become more inclined to sell and buyers become less inclined to buy as the price advances towards resistance. It is believed that by the time the price reaches the level of resistance, supply will overcome demand and prevent the price from rising above resistance.

Now that you have a basic understanding of candlestick charts, we're going to discuss the value of looking for patterns of the regular charts. We know every candlestick on the daily charts represents one day of price action. Whenever I transact I usually look at the daily charts for about 3-6 months of trading history. I hold a regular graphic for every stock that I sell. Note, as a day trader, our primary focus will be on finding patterns on charts between 1min and 5min. Both intraday maps still occur inside their daily chart, though. This means that we need to keep an eye on the daily support and resistance levels that might come into play nearby. Both maps will have help and resistance price rates and it's important to know how to define certain levels. Given that professional traders must value the critical support and resistance rates, if you don't know where they are, you can end up buying when and where everyone else is selling. A method of technical analysis is to map the price history on stock charts. Unlike fundamental analyzes where we position trades dependent on a firm's power, technical traders base trades on chart patterns and readings of indicators. We are searching for fundamental breakout trends as competitive day traders. Recall that volume will always ensure that the breakout is true. The escape typically won't be managed without length.

I firmly believe a great daily chart will provide day traders with configurations that have potential for home run. Notwithstanding a weak daily chart with a lot of resistance, I've seen thousands of stocks making incredible intraday movements too. This will arise when there is such a heavy stimulus that it overrides any amount of regular resistance. Picture, for instance, a prescription stock that has a lot of regular resistance, but has just discovered the solution for an incurable disease before. The news is so fantastic that as markets rush to get a piece of the action, the daily chart becomes almost insignificant. This is a good time to remind you that stocks can be either weak or irrationally high! Often inventories are far beyond what the company's fundamental analysis might be able to project. It indicates a disconnection between a stock's dynamics and its actual behavior. We need to act like a dealer, and concentrate on trading the trends of the map. If a stock appears to display bullish feelings and has no sign of reversal, there is no reason to sell a long position or launch a reversal trade. While we will review the important levels on daily charts you need to understand, it is also important to remember that a strong catalyst typically overrides a weak daily chart. Conversely, despite a strong daily chart, a good intraday catalyst can rarely break out, because a poor catalyst results in low volume and loss of retail value. The strongest breakouts come with high relative value, and there will be no exchange if there is no quantity.

Recent Support and Resistance Levels

Levels of support and resistance are formed when a stock touches a price repeatedly, and can not break that price. When this happens downside we call that a level of support. When it occurs upside down we term it a degree of resistance. The more times a stock touches the level without breaking it, the more the support and resistance levels gain validity. If you pull up a daily chart for any stock you should be able to draw horizontal lines in which you can see critical levels that traders respect. Occasionally a level breaks briefly, and then prices swiftly reverse. This is regarded as a manufactured escape. Day traders must be very cautious of fake breakouts, because we often take positions before the breakout is verified. When we delay until we have assurance to take our place, the breakout has already started and we will have missed a lot of the opportunity for benefit. For this purpose, learning to predict possible breakouts and learning to recognize indicators of a false breakout for any trader will be an important skill. Alternatively we will establish a long or short bias on each of the stocks on our morning watch list by knowing the level of support and resistance. This will help to determine the value of the markets and the kind of configurations that you are searching for.

Daily Chart of Gapper - Marking Out Recent Price Levels of Possible Support/Resistance.

As I look at the stocks traded on an above average volume each morning, I like to look at the daily chart to identify areas of support or resistance nearby. Looking back at previous support or resistance levels, you have to remember that the level is only valid if the price hasn't been broken since the day it was made high or low. Which ensures if a candle had a maximum of $10.00 two months ago, and a candle rendered a high of $10.10 yesterday, the high of $10.00 no longer applies. That high had been broken. If a stock runs up I'm going to look for the next obvious point of resistance. It usually takes the form of a candle's high or small. I'm going to highlight each of these recent prices, so if I decide to take a day's trade, I'm going to be aware of potential rates where sellers could keep back the price. It gives me a sense of increased potential if there is no resistance on a map but only if the catalyst is solid.

Ascending and Descending Support and Resistance Lines

In addition to horizontal lines of support and resistance, we will draw lines of support and resistance both ascending and falling. Such curves are not always as clear as the degrees of horizontality. As they're less obvious, traders also don't always respect them well. Each time I draw trend lines on a map, I want to draw them at what seems to be the most obvious place. That means we need to see lots of candles tapping the trend line and validating it. My maps usually have a number of horizontal lines at recent areas of help and opposition, including one or two upward or downward trend lines centered on the broad movement of the last few months. Occasionally, during the creation of a pullback I may draw a downward trend line, or to illustrate the top or bottom of a flag sequence. Typically these types of trend lines span the duration of just a few days of price action.

Windows and Triggers

As I glance at the regular maps, I search for gaps that do not have help and opposition. I realize we have breakout potential when the price action gets inside that window and the price that push to the top or bottom of that window. It is important to note that we want only stocks which have breakout potential to be exchanged. If an asset has the potential to move $1.00, then we could grab just half of the transfer. So it's not worth watching if a stock doesn't have the potential to make a big move. Those openings we're searching for must be extremely obvious to get the relatively high volume required to get a big move. Based on the strategies I trade, windows and triggers are only in play on stocks which due to a catalyst have a high relative price. For this reason I don't spend much time looking despite openings and causes on the random stock regular maps. I'm just reviewing market indexes that are in operation every day as a consequence of reporting.

What is the gap between degree of a stimulus and level of resistance? A trigger technically is a potential level of resistance, but the difference between calling it resistance and calling it a trigger is based on how much room it has until the next level of resistance. A level of resistance which has a large window no resistance above it is called a trigger. A range on a map must be greater than the stock's Average True Range (ATR) to allow it relevant to me. Growing stock has an average true value, depending on the last 14 days ' price range. If a product has an ATR of 50 million, this means it travels 50 dollars per day on average. I would consider it a trigger if I looked at that stock's daily chart and noticed a resistance price for 75 cents that didn't have another resistance level above it. If that catalyst will smash the mark, there is room for a move up to the next point. On the other side, if you find a price level with another 10 cents resistance level and another 10 cents resistance level, these are all small areas of resistance. There are no stimuli, because the price levels are too closely packed together. The best daily charts will have large windows at the top and bottom of each window with major causes. Long body candles or holes can be the space which produces the windows. Those are the only two ways of creating a view on a map.

Gaps

If you look at nearly any of the chart, you'll see gaps. These are the days where stock was sold either higher or lower than the previous day of exchange. Gap days are triggered by some form of structural stimulus like results, a press release or some other big news item. We know we're usually going to trade stocks on the gap days, but it's also important to understand how those big gaps can be

Support and Resistance at Whole Dollars and Half Dollars

Besides the levels of support and resistance we will see trend lines, openings, or holes from rising or falling, we will also see help and resistance when stocks hit entire dollars and half dollars. A stock that reaches thresholds such as $10.00, $10.50, $11.00, and so on will usually face opposition at those whole and half dollar points. Conversely, a stock that sells off may find support as it falls to entire dollars and half dollars. I try to take entries between whole dollar and half dollar marks whenever feasible, because I can usually set my stop on the other side of that price level. If conventional chart patterns match with whole dollars and half dollars, the design is granted tremendous energy. Stocks priced below $10.00 will often find it harder to break through those critical levels than stocks priced higher. A break of a whole dollar, like $3.00, could be an opportunity to take a long stand with a $2.90 or $2.95 stop. Stocks of all price ranges are adapting well to whole dollars and half dollars demand help and resistance.

Usually, if I'm in a long position and a stock is hitting a whole dollar, I'm starting to take income in the.90s, before it meets pressure, then keeping the rest with a pause at breakeven. I'd expect prices to tap the entire dollar to test the level of resistance, and then pull back. The touch sometimes becomes the peak of the day, and the pattern reverses. When I reach a market at $9.99, I use a close 10-cent pause in expectation of the whole dollar split, because I'm heading into a stock below the tops. When rates break over the whole dollar, it is very critical that it remains above the actual dollar. If rates push through the level of resistance and then break back down, I will sometimes use this as an opportunity to take a short position with a stop of 10 cent. Investing above and below the whole dollar and half dollar can provide the potential for fantastic entrants on both trend investing and reversal. Because the entrants are often in expectation of breakouts or reversals, trading around whole dollars brings a bit more risk than conventional chart patterns. I still keep tight stops on those trades for this reason. It is important to note that all-dollar and half-dollar trade is only relevant on stocks traded on high relative turnover or intraday intense trading.

Moving Average Support and Resistance

Both daily charts and intraday charts respect moving averages. When a weak stock gaps up it's not uncommon for the price to open around moving average resistance. Even though the stock has gapped up, it will struggle with the daily resistance levels unless the catalyst is particularly strong. I typically look to trade stocks in the direction of the daily trend. A stock gapping up should be breaking up and away from its moving averages just as a stock gapping down should be breaking down and away from its moving averages. We can use the information of daily windows and gaps, the levels of trend line support, and the position of the moving averages to help us create our long or short bias against a stock. This becomes the basis for how we will trade the stock.

On an intraday level moving averages present one of the most signiÀcant forms of support and resistance. It's very common to see trending stocks respecting the support of moving averages. It's important to recognize this support because if we have a long bias we can use moving average pullbacks as entry opportunities. Often times these pullbacks will also take the familiar form of a bull Áag. In addition to noting the importance of moving average support and resistance, it's important to be mindful of when price crosses moving averages. If the price has been respecting the 9 EMA all day long and suddenly crosses below it, there could be an opportunity for a trend reversal. We will cover the details of these trading strategies later on, but for now I'd encourage you to keep a close eye on how stocks trade around their moving averages.

CHAPTER 6: TREND (MOMENTUM) TRADING STRATEGIES

I want to explore seeking your entry now that you have a solid understanding of help and opposition, simple chart settings and how to pick stocks that are worth trading. That's where the road meets the rubber. We should address chart patterns and configurations as well as ways to reach the right type of stock while managing risk and reducing losses. I describe the setup of a chart as having a safe chance to get into a strong stock. You can notice that some of the trends we study seem somewhat mysterious, but I promise you that the more you look at maps, the more they are evident. If we sell, we always want to go back to taking simple configurations, because that implies that more people are likely to purchase at the same breakout locations. The most important thing to remember about momentum trading is that it will always give you the lowest risk and the highest reward potential to enter close to support. Usually this means buying near-moving average support or pullback at the bottom of a bull flag. Although purchasing near-high-of-day stocks will work in competitive markets, it is also a higher risk approach. Alternatively, we should concentrate on pullback entries that arise when a chart pattern is created, commonly known as a flag.

You need to say you can explain the danger if you consider taking a deal. Which ensures you have to consider what the real risk is. My favorite trends all have well-defined support levels that we use as the price of the total failure. We take the loss and move on if the stock breaks below that support level. My place size will be dependent on the difference between my entrance and the stop and how much money I'm willing to risk in the exchange. Once I have defined my risk, I need to subtract my danger by two as my benefit goal. That will earn me the 2:1 profit loss which is crucial as a trader to long-term success. With loads of prompts and openings, we have already addressed the added value of solid regular maps, and the effectiveness of a successful intraday stimulus. We will extend the chart patterns in this chapter only to the powerful stocks that we consider worthy of trading. Chart patterns on low stocks are of no interest to us.

My primary approaches are long-range, momentum trading strategies. During the pre-market session I love to find a stock that has a perfect trigger with lots of windows on the daily chart. Over the years we've seen some impressive changes from the influence titles. One of the largest in recent memory was from a market that started at $18.00 and reached a $55.00 peak within 60 minutes of trading. When stocks make those kinds of intraday movements, it is a reminder never to underestimate market strength. I also buy stocks as a momentum investor which have already made a big leap. As a buyer, purchasing a stock that has just moved up 5-10 percent would not make much sense, but as a day trader, we realize we can handle our risk based on the level of intraday support and try to ride the spike for another 5-10 percent. It is uncommon for stocks under $10 to create intraday moves of 50 per cent when there is a cause or high relative demand.

I use Limit Orders to get into and exit my positions for all of my trading strategies. I purchase at the Ask price, and typically always try to sell at the Ask level. I regularly transact through my brokerage account using the Level2 (market depth) slot. Learning Level2 is very essential for day traders, particularly when using a fast paced strategy such as the strategy for gap and go. When we analyze the following techniques, you'll find me explaining the strategy of half sales (scaling out) and changing my stops to breakeven. One of the reasons I have a high percentage of profitability is because I take off the table a little as soon as I hit my first profit target, then change my stop loss to breakeven. Unless I end up getting barred from trading, with a small profit, I'll still be walking away from trade. If the stock continues to run, I can let it ride knowing that I've already locked a winner and that there's anything else on the cake to be icing. It is important to keep at least a small place in the trade until an exit sign prevents me from doing so. It means that, without leaving too early, I exchanged the stock from start to finish and it helps me to have some pretty big winners. As regards losses, it is even more important to cap all your losses at the predetermined maximum loss. I know the price when I enter a trade, where I'll stop for a loss. Remember, a gambler is thinking about profits but about risk (loss) things for a trader. When we are dealing, we must always stick to our roots as risk managers.

Momentum Trading Strategy

Recall one of the first items I mentioned was that we are value hunters as day traders. Momentum inventories are guided by distance. The configurations for the Momentum technique include Bull Flags, Bear Flags, Flat Top Breakouts, Flat Bottom Breakdowns, Moving Average Pullbacks, and Parabolic Movers. It is possible to trade momentum to both the long side and the short side. Almost always the most competitive fluid markets will have weak floats. I see a small market stock as seeing securities below 50 million. Typically, the best low float competitors have a float of less than 10 million shares. Such products have a very small trading stock supply. Under the right circumstances, a high level of demand can create a powerful squeeze where in a matter of minutes a stock will rise 100 per cent. On a market with a 100 million share float this sort of change could never happen. You will make a determination on the prospects for a deal by understanding the flow. Seeing opportunity is significant, as it allows us to justify the risk of taking the trade first. Whether we search at benefit goals on momentum transactions, they will often be focused on the level of resistance in the daily chart, but they will also be affected by the market, the cause, and volume rates. Past riders, low float stocks will always have more capacity than a high flow volume.

Every day I start by running my stock scanners to find pre-market stocks. Thanks to a trigger of some kind such stocks are already traded on strong pre-market volume. I'm creating a four to six of those stocks watch list. During the day, I keep running motivation stock scanners to seek out new ideas. During the day, the scanners I run look for stocks that hit a new high of day on a relative volume above average. All the inventories that reach the scanner have promise, but it is the trader's job to find the best prospects.

Buying the First and Second Pullbacks

Every time a dynamic stock breaks out, I will look to trade the breakout as well as trade the first and second pullback potentially. Such pullbacks can be a bull signal, a flat top breakdown, or a moving average retracement. The best pullbacks are a flag of the bull which touches the EMA 9. We will discuss each of these patterns in detail below. It is important to understand why stocks react well to both the first and second pullbacks. It's because traders missing the first breakout will often try to purchase the first pullback, and some traders missing the first pullback will trade the second pullback, especially if the stock shows extreme strength. Again, if the relative volume is extremely high, we can confirm there is strength. It becomes much riskier to take entrants beyond the second pullback unless the market goes through a phase of restructuring. But with that said, if a stock seems to be irrationally heavy, which they are often, then I can continue to trade beyond the second pullback. In these situations, I will use smaller sizes of place to avoid the first trades from returning income. If the market allows a fresh breakout after a long period of stagnation, we will sell the breakout again, and the first and second pullbacks. On both the five minute chart and the one minute chart we look for pullbacks.

Flat Top Breakouts (Ascending Wedge)

We're going to start with my favorite design, the flat top breakout. I respect flat top breakouts because they're extremely bullish, leaving little room to get the breakout location correctly. On any time frame, a flat top breakout may occur, but they are typically the strongest on the 5-minute chart. A flat top breakout trend allows a stock to have in the last few hours, usually 4 percent or more, made a strong move up. The stock trades sideways just below a resistance level, rather than pulling back or selling off after the strong move. The consolidation period whilst forming the flat top can be as short as three to five minutes, or as long as several hours. The strongest flat top breakout trends are consolidating below an entire dollar point or a half dollar. We know stocks frequently find resistance around these price levels, so consolidation is ideal in that area. It is critical that the stock keeps making slightly higher lows during the time of restructuring, without it making higher highs. Which generates an increasing level of support. When I enter a pattern of flat top breakout my stop is just below the trend line of ascending support. When the price finally breaks above the point of resistance, we expect an immediate volume explosion. The jump in price suggests that thousands of other traders followed the trend and waited for a breakthrough before purchasing their stock. Retesting the breakout price immediately after the breakdown isn't rare for the level. This is a re-testof previous support rates at that stage. If the amount remains, assistance has become previous opposition and we should see a continuation of the rally.

If a flat top breakout configuration is emerging, I should look at the daily chart as soon as possible to see if we have any openings or triggers nearby. If a flat top breakout has been consolidating on my stock scanners for several hours, it is unlikely I will see it. This is because the day isn't going to hit high. Typically I would only notice these long consolidation setups if I watched the stock already, because it had a high relative volume. Remember that only stocks with high relative volume should be traded on flat top breakout patterns. If I sell flat top breakouts, I typically buy right at the point of peak. The apex point is the flat top's highest price, and is the price of resistance. That price is the breakout price, to the penny. We expect a rapid surge in buying and short coverage when the price breaks that level. I am watching Level2 as the stock approaches with my order the breakout price, ready to buy just before break. If I begin to see a surge in buying volume going through time and sales, and I see the seller sitting on the Ask and buying up, I'll jump in with a half-sized order. Picking a flat top breakout means buying up a stock at day's big. That's a bit risky, which is why I'm beginning at half scale. My stop will be at the bottom of the wedge, the ascending support line. If on the first attempt the stock fails to break out, I can hang on unless my stop is turned off. If the stock succeeds in breaking over the top of the fiat but then immediately falls back below the price of the breakout, I will sell for a loss before my stop is touched. I would sell half of my stake once I have made a return equivalent to my expense if the price spikes up. I then change my stop to breakeven and hold the rest of the spot until an escape signal prevents me.

If I am confident I can add to my position during the first or second pullback after breakout. Some traders who skipped the initial breakout should take advantage of the first and second pullbacks as their buying opportunity. That's why the first and second pullbacks are often brought up on the bursting of solid momentum markets. If I've already sold half of my stake for a boost, I'll add back the stock I sold at the pullback breakout stage. Then I'll adjust my stop to the pullback low which leaves me with a profitable trade, even if I'm stopped. The first and second pullback may appear on a one-minute map, and can take the form of a bull flag or even a flat top breakup. A flat top breakout can be sold on the five-minute monitor, and a bull flag or flat top breakout can also be exchanged on the one-minute board.

Flat Bottom Breakdowns

The fiat down collapse is the opposite to the flat top breakup. We have the same opportunity as a flat top breakout when a stock is very weak and consolidating near the lows, just above a critical support level. With low risk entry there is the opportunity for a quick profit. As with any other system, we want to do our due diligence to evaluate the driver in action, search for support / resistance areas in the daily chart, and make sure we can achieve at least a 2:1 benefit loss ratio. They focus this on the first goal for benefit and the distance from a reasonable stop

Bull Flags

Bull flags are my second favorite design on paper. A bull flag resembles a flat top escape, except for one very important difference. Unlike a flat top breakup, the first strong move will include a bull flag feeling a minor pullback. I noticed that some of my biggest winning trades are created by bull flags out of all the setups I trade. The only explanation I like flat top breakouts is because the flat top indicates a better bullish mood, because there was no pull back on the stock. A traditional bull flag can have three to five strong, long body green candles push, and then have one to three smaller red candles pulling back. While on every time frame bull flags can be exchanged, I like the one minute charts and the five minutes charts. We typically look for bull flags on stocks that are already on our watch list, because we know that because of a catalyst they're going to trade with heavy volume. I also notice bull flags by monitoring the energy scans early in the day. Stocks that are rising with a high relative volume, when they start pullback, can form bull flags worth trade. It places me in the traders community who skipped the first push but will purchase the first and second pullbacks. More than 25 per cent of the transfer will take back the best bull flags. Unlike a flat top breakout when we purchase at the consolidation point, we buy during a bull flag when the first candle is making a new peak. A potential turning point when energy moves back into the bulls ' hands is called the first candle to make a new peak over the maximum of a previous candle. I place my stop loss at the low of the pullback when I join on the first candle to make a new peak, and have my first profit target at the high of the day range.

It's critical that we don't get into the bull flags at daytime big. Many novice traders would misinterpret a bull signal for a flat top breakout and hesitate to purchase until it hits the high day mark. Normally a double top is created when a stock takes a quick move up, a pullback, and then a second step upwards. Triple tops are always to be strong points of resistance. Remember that for the resistance price a flat top consists of three or more taps. If a stock is extremely strong it can break through the double top resistance and keep running, but the difference between a flat top breakout and a double top after a bull flag is important to recognize. Normally buying double tops means buying a stock at the height of the day, and then having to sell it for a loss. A double top often transforms into a flat top breakup pattern if enough time is given to integrate.

High volume during the initial move higher, low volume during the pullback and then high volume as the stock goes up and down the rises is an important characteristic to look for on the bull Á ag. If you see high volume on the pullback, it may be an indication that the market may eventually be reversal, rather than setting up higher for a second move. The high volume amount on the pullback indicates that short sellers may be joining the exchange to drive it lower.

Bear Flags

The opposite of a bull flag is a bear banner. We are looking for a strong sell off, a small rebound on light volume and then the first candle that will make a new low to launch the next sale round. I sell flat bottom breakdowns, but I generally don't exchange bear flags unless they're particularly evident. If I sell bear flags, they are usually flags that appear on a one-minute chart due to a sudden price decline. If news breaks and a stock declines 5 per cent instantly, they sometimes bounce up briefly, until they fall off again. The strongest sell flags are the ones that appear on volume-booming stocks.

A stock that has been generally weak throughout the day and on the five-minute chart is developing a longer bear flag can be a good candidate for a fade day. These are products that may not have headlines, but will just grind down on price. If a stock on lighter demand creates a bear flag, it is important to remember that the overall market strength or weakness will affect the price. Since I'm mostly cynical for a long time, I prefer taking extremely obvious configurations if I decide to make short stocks.

Moving Average Retracements

It's no longer a bull sign at a certain stage after a stock has made a quick move up, then pulls back more than three or five candles. A bull flag needs a very distinctive overhead push, and a brief pullback time before attempting another upward move. This is neither a bull signal nor a flat top breakout sequence when a stock pulls back and consolidates through pullback. It is literally a sequence of flags. If I look at flag trends, I like seeing the stock stabilize past 9 EMA support or maybe 20 EMA support. Moving average retracements will almost always be focused on the five-minute map, as they are slower moving setups which allow more traders to note. We just swap configurations of one minute on fast moving breakouts. The explanation I like the moving average retracements is because it's a good indicator of power in the cycle as values stay above the 9 EMA. When a stock has pulled back beyond a traditional bull sign, I normally wait until the price actually hits the 9 EMA before I take my stance. In the event a stock has pulled back and disrupted the foundation of the bull flag, we can not purchase the first candle to make a new high any more. Instead we have to wait for the consolidation of the moving average. Heavy stocks often ride the 9 EMA for a duration of several hours. Any pullback to the 9 EMA offers those types of trending stocks a low-risk entry opportunity.

I should purchase during a 9-EMA pullback once the market has reached the 9 EMA and place my stop at the pullback limit or just below the moving average. Usually, I like to see the price hitting the 9 EMA, then start curling slowly before I take my place. It suggests to me that traders value the moving average as a level of support. Note, the distinction between the bull flag and the 9 EMA pullback is that it normally takes a long time to create the 9 EMA pullback. If I hold a position from a 9 EMA pullback system, I'm going to sell half through the day spike and change my breakeven stop. Until I see an escape sign, I must keep the remaining position.

Most cautious traders are going to use a tactic to join just trades close to moving average help. Entering near-moving average support for trend-based trades offers the lowest risk entry. Plus, many of these players may hold positions until the price action hits a moving average. In MRTX's stock chart, you can easily see that if you joined on the first moving average pullback after the trend picked up at 11:20am, you'd be in at about $37.00. You could have held that position until around 3:30pm, when the price fell at $41.00 below the EMA 9. This is a good approach as these forms of transactions will offer an opportunity to engage in the business without having to participate in high speed trading. Slower moving trend based trades are generally suited for smaller share size due to increased risk of exposure time.

Regarding low stocks we may exchange even transfer average retracements to the short side. On the 9 EMA pop the rules for shorting weak stocks are the same as the 9 EMA pullback trade. Moving average entries provide short opportunities that I find far safer than a traditional bear flag because they are less volatile and slower moving. The moving average support gives me trust in the trend whether to the long or the short side.

Buying a Higher High after a Pullback during a Five Minute Uptrend

We see various configurations during the consolidation phase when a pullback is emerging, depending on which map we are looking at. While checking for configurations, I still turn to the Five Minute Map. We would aim for a pullback entry when we have a stock that has offered us a long bias on the daily chart, and we have a strong trend on the 5 minute map. In the case of the example above on CTRV, you can see that the price pulled back below the one minute moving averages on the one minute chart. The stock pulls back to price (1), then pivots to price (2), then pivots again to price (3). It's important to note that the (3) pullback was a price higher than (1). This is relevant because the demand could have been smaller than the market threshold (1), and a short-term substitution would have proceeded. During this time we can see that the price hit the 9 EMA on the five minute map. The pivot at price (2), to reach this location, is the spot we need to see crack. A market break (2) would show on the one-minute map that the pattern is being revived as the price is higher. The fact that the price break (2) will also be the first five-minute candle to make a new high is what makes this pattern particularly strong on the one minute. I still watch the one-minute charts as well as the five-minute charts and search for them to send me the same market entry signals. The price will be the point of peak where a trend bursts out or breaks down.

Parabolic Moves

We love as day traders when markets shift in parabolic fashions. A parabolic step is when a stock simply goes straight up or down. Almost always this trend is the product of an effective stimulus and a solid regular map. Stocks that will be irrationally strong or weak are parabolic movers. We saw stocks losing half their value in one day, while others are increasing by more than 1000%. Such kinds of dramatic moves are not rare in today's markets.

There are several ways parabolic movers can be exchanged. If I want to share in the rally, I'll join parabolic stocks in the shape of a bull flag or a flat top breakout on a momentary pullback. Such trends should usually be on the one minute chart since the stock travels very quickly. I'll enjoy the momentum as much as possible if I can get an entry, but I'll make sure that I sell half of my stake immediately and change my stop to breakeven. Getting up quickly is not unusual, and then watching the price drop right back to breakeven or a loss. Buying a parabolic mover involves basically still chasing, so running may be risky. By using smaller roles, we have to mitigate the risk inherent in selling these forms of stocks until we have built on the name a profit margin and can afford to take a greater risk.

The second approach to exchange parabolic stocks is to wait before the turnaround takes place. We can't always make the entry period or foresee when a stock will run 100 percent, but at some stage we assume that almost all major moves will be reversed. The challenge is that some securities will appear like they're about to reverse when they're up to 100%, but instead they end up running at 200%. It can be as risky to try and predict the top or bottom of a parabolic step as to follow the momentum. As we have already said, day-trading is hazardous, but by eliminating the most volatile configurations, we can mitigate risk. Parabolic movers are the highest risk setups that we will be debating. We offer high challenges but good prospects for profit. Generally, when selling such kinds of securities as a risk reduction technique, I reduce my share size. If I will try to take up a reversal trade, I will always continue with a quarter of the size of my intended place. It helps the stock to keep squeezing up, without preventing me. We might have the right idea but it's the wrong timing. The advantage of scaling in is that we don't need to pick the exact counterpoint. We can add a quarter size, add another quarter and then add full size once confirmed by the reversal. The downside in scaling in is that once a turnaround is verified, because of the size of parabolic stocks we will often be really far away from the halt. If you trade parabolic stocks with momentum setups, reversal setups or both, note that it's simple to worry of all the opportunities for gains and forget about risk control as stocks continue to rise. I still try to stay focused on my level of risk and use smaller roles to minimize the passions and ambition involved in big movers.

Entering a Momentum Trade

When I'm preparing to enter a momentum trade, I pull Level 2 up and look at the spreads and volume amount first. I will usually like to see small spreads of 5 cents or fewer. A stock of big spreads will be harder to manage, because they can rise or drop easily without allowing anyone time to get out.

One Minute Entries

Many of my Momentum Trading Strategies involve purchasing trends centered on one minute map. We require enormously high relative volume to take a one-minute setup. We need so much volume that the five minute candles are too big to use to manage the risk. I still have an exact price in mind as I reach a deal that I want to purchase at. The price is usually the apex of the pattern, this is the top of the one-minute candle in the case of a one-minute Gap and Go ORB. This is the quality of the flat peak in the event of a Flat Peak Breakout. In my brokerage account, I plan my limit order, with a few cents offset above the level, and then watch Level2. I will normally get filled by using a small offset. If I see a strong amount of resistance at the level I want to buy, I'll wait until that seller starts moving or the shares get bought before pressing the purchasing button. I move in just before it feels like the price is about to fall. Because I purchase most of my momentum trades at the peak stage, I anticipate resolution to be almost instantaneous. If I don't see instant progress, it's a sign of vulnerability by itself, and a warning to possibly reduce my scale or leave altogether. I always start with a half-sized position, using the one-minute chart. When I buy at the apex point, I never like to start with the full size, because if I'm wrong, I'm going to experience a huge loss. Furthermore, I'm subjected at my highest risk level if I first start a deal. Alternatively, if I can change my stop to breakeven I continue with half size and double it up. When I can't double up, I'll happily take the win with the smaller size of the place realizing that I handled my chance correctly.

Five Minute Entries

Since I have more faith in five minute trends, on my first order I would typically take on a larger size. I'm always purchasing the pinnacle of the trend of five minute chart patterns, the bull flag breaking point or the peak of the flat top breakup. The only configurations I could use on the five-minute map in the case of Gap and Go trades would be the five-minute ORB, the first pullback or a Red to Green transfer. Most of my Gap and Go trades continue with first entry on the one-minute table. On the five minute chart, midday momentum trading of strong stocks will typically form patterns. Midday is a bad time to trade off the one-minute table, as the amount is usually much lower than the first trading hour. I typically use the five minute chart for momentum trades past 10 AM unless there is breaking news or extremely heavy volume. Depending on the setup, when I jump in, I immediately set my stop at the low of the pullback, just below the 9 EMA or just below the upward support line.

Profit Targets Trades can be incredibly fast. I was in stocks that in a matter of minutes grew by 50 percent and then dropped back all the way down and finished the red day. It ensures I can sell half my stake whenever I am up the value I lost on the exchange. I may hold the position a little longer before scaling out on momentum trades that have the ideal set of entry requirements, with a good daily chart and a strong catalyst. Instead, I would change my stop to breakeven whether I join a momentum trade on a one-minute setup with the intention of doubling on the five-minute validation, or the high day break like on a bull flag. I no longer run the risk of losing money on the exchange as

I double up. Whenever I can get a breakeven pause in a deal, I'm in the drivers ' seat. I got a free chance to win a big winner.

It can be difficult to estimate benefit expectations on the momentum trades. We are hoping for a bounce back up to the 9 EMA or the VWAP with reversal trades, but with momentum trades we have to look at the daily chart or check for technical areas of resistance. We consider resistance usually about half dollars and whole dollars ($10.00, $10.50, $11.00, etc.). If I'm in a momentum trade and it's approaching a point of reasonable resistance, I try to take benefit. So I change my breakeven stop or move my stop into the benefit sector. I always want to hold a partial stake before I quit, so I can feel that from start to finish I have sold the stock properly. Selling for a small profit, and then seeing a stock pass without you, is always frustrating. I don't transform momentum trades into swing trades, because it's usually not a good idea to hold overnight when a market is up 20-30 per cent intraday. They will sometimes keep on going, but the danger is too high to justify the incentive.

Exit Indicators

When I see any of the following performance indications, I shall leave my position immediately:

1. I scaled out of half my place a five minute candle making a new low BEFORE (five minute candles making a new low can suggest a potential reversal).

2. Price breaks on Chart 3 of five minutes below the 9 EMA.

3. I adjusted my stop to breakeven and stop.

I learned to follow a handful of reliable exit indicators when I traded momentum. If I am in a transaction and see an exit sign, I close my position immediately, regardless of the overall profit or loss. I found that waiting to hit my stop after seeing an exit indicator only serves to make the loss bigger. Trading is about capping our costs. That means you take the hint and move on to the next chance as soon as a trade gives you a reason to exit.

The first exit signal is a new low five-minute light, until I scaled out of half my place. I'm willing to hold through a five-minute candle making a new low once I'm in the driver's seat and have sold half my place and changed my pause to breakeven. I can end up holding a second bull flag by shaping it, and be able to ride the momentum. I will remain in the place as long as the price doesn't come down to my entry price.

The second predictor of exit is a demand fall below the EMA 9. If I've scaled out or I'm keeping my full position, if the market falls below the 9 EMA, I have to leave the trade and take whatever profit or loss I can. I use the 9 EMA to gage pattern power. High momentum stocks are likely to trade along the 9 EMA, moving up and down, before consolidating back near the moving average. Stocks will run for the whole day without breaching the EMA 9. By using a 9 EMA break as my last exit signal, I have the ability to maintain a partial spot for hours while a stock keeps running. That's how you make big winners.

When my stop price is activated, the final predictor is. Originally my stop price would have been focused on either my overall risk or a limited level of support. When exchange advances, then I change my stops to breakeven, then into the benefit sector. By holding that final position until my stop was fired, it ensured that without selling too soon, I traded the full range.

CHAPTER 7: COUNTER TREND (REVERSAL) TRADING STRATEGIES

I am a big fan of price reversals as well as flipping momentum securities to the upside. One of the first items I learned as a young trader was that, when a stock is going to make a big change upside down or sideways, it's impossible to predict, but almost all of those moves can end in a reversal. Instead of feeling frustrated that I was missing a big mover, I saw it as a chance to exchange the turnaround. The challenge is to find the turnaround and not get into storage heading too early in the wrong direction. Many counter-trend traders are experiencing large losses because they too soon begin to enter reversal positions. Because countertrend trading involves guessing the pattern transition, it is obviously harder than momentum trading. The big advantage in reversal trading is that you'll have an outstanding profit-loss ratio anytime you purchase a bad stock really close to the bottom. The cost in comparison to the profit potential is almost always very small, because your stop is at daytime high or day low. We have already learned that having a profit loss ratio of 2:1 means that you can be a profitable trader with a success rate of just 50 per cent. I often get 3:1 profit-loss ratios on reversal trades. I'll end at the low of the day for 10-15 cents, and get 50 cents of benefit off the bounce. Such forms of benefit risk ratios mean that even if the levels of success is smaller, you can afford to take on more risks as the winners usually exceed the losers by far.

Only Trading Extremes

Reversal setups ought to be either at high of day or low of day, with at least 3-5 consecutive long body candles, while 5-10 is preferable. The last candle in the series of successive candles should be a candle outside the Bollinger bands. A candle beyond the bands of the Bollinger is a conclusive predictor of intense motion. Furthermore, I search for the Relative Strength Index to prove the market is either over 80 (overbought) or below 20 (oversold). I need more indications than an instant exchange, since reversals are difficult to properly time.

The Reversal Bar

Our reversal bar will be our last candle in the show. The right reversal bar is entirely outside the Bollinger bands, and should preferably assume the shape of a doji, a top or bottom handle, or a hammer or reversed ax. The candlestick is our key candle which we will use to establish our price of entry and exit. We will shorten the first five minute candle in the case of a top reversal to make a new low versus the low of the trigger candle. Our stop is going to be cause candle big. I have to change my size according to the level of risk between my admission and the price of the rest.

Alignment with the daily chart Although countertrend trades can be profitable without running into daily chart support or resistance, many of the best setups for reversal will have confirmation on the daily chart. The daily confirmation helps to justify the reversal point, meaning more traders will take part in the reversal trade. As we learned from our earlier lecture, greater volume generally means better resolution. The point of reversal on the daily chart can be to reach a critical area of assistance or opposition, or to crash into a moving average. Typically the obvious daily levels will provide more support than the obscure levels.

Volume While volume on reversals is not as critical as that on momentum transactions, I still like to see high relative volume. Some of the strongest reversal trades on the last candle should witness the highest volume of the day, prior to the reversal. When this happens, it is called the top volume, or the bottom volume. We need the high volume on momentum trades to insure the breakout occurs. When the sea turns after an intense sell off, the stock will move back on lighter volume toward the VWAP with reversal trades. As a general rule of thumb, to find a reversal deal, I need to see at least 500,000 in volume on a day. If we deal in lighter volume reversals we need to be particularly aware of the overall market impact. When the economy as a whole is really low, certain securities will show as potential candidates for turnaround, as they sell off in tandem with the sector. If the economy does indeed rebound, these stocks will often recover perfectly, but if the market continues to sell, such stocks will be pulled back.

Deep Industry There are occasions when a whole industry is very broad to the upside or downside. Stocks that appear on our reversal scanner may meet the technical requirements for a reversal, but may not always be appropriate for trade. We have to be careful about taking reversal trades during a day when a whole market is low. Nevertheless, if the total market begins reversing, any of the stocks on the reversal scanner can be exchanged as out of the hundreds of stocks in the business, those stocks fit our criteria the most. I will often select several stocks on the scanner in the same sector and try to catch a market-wide turnaround through several stocks. Even if the market is reversing, certain stocks are going to reverse with greater strength than others.

Reversal Conditions to Enter:

1. 3 + Five-minute, continuous candles

2. Candles are running the bands Bollinger or outside the bands Bollinger

3. Stock is at Day 1, or Day 4

4. RSI is above 80 and under 20

5. Float is not usually a concern here, but should be remembered before reaching position

6. Ideally, one of our favorite reversal candles is the final candle

7. Ideally, we bounce off resistance everyday

8. Ideally our judgment is influenced by the overall market.

9. You need a 2:1 profit loss ratio 10 to be able to reasonably accomplish. The five minute map shall contain at least 30 cents to the EMA9

Entering a Reversal Trade

When I'm preparing to enter a reversal deal, I bring Level 2 up and look at the spreads (the difference between the bid and the request) and check the volume level. If the stock fits all my entry requirements, I'll take a position and set out either a 20 cent stop or a stop at day's high or low instantly. I usually execute a quarter-or half-sized reversal exchange. I may have the right idea like parabolic trades but the wrong timing. I can allow a little more room for the stock to move before stopping me at my maximum loss by starting with smaller size. I'm going to exit if a stock drops to a new high or new low, but as long as the price is between my entrance and the stop I'm going to hold on.

One Minute Entry

I also use my first quarter size position to make a new high dependent on the first one minute candle, if there are at least 10 consecutive one minute candles. I usually try to enter a one-minute chart-based reversal trade with the first spot, and then if I'm successful and we get five-minute approval I'll increase my place to the full size. Looking at the one-minute chart I may decide to take my first place before the five-minute confirmation if I see the stock reaching a level of regular resistance. Since we know stocks vary around whole dollars and half dollars in help and opposition, I will sometimes look to buy a bad stock if I see it falling below a whole dollar, like $50.00. Then I'll get it if that entire dollar comes back up. If it is able to reclaim the whole dollar's money, that is often a secure entrance with a $49.90 exit. If the stock breaks through a price of $50.00, I would shorten it as it breaks down below the whole dollar, with a pause at $50.10. Such one-minute interventions will give me a great average pretty similar to the high of the day or the low of the day, but if the reverse does not work, I will be ready to bail out. Since trade reversals on the one-minute chart are riskier, I use smaller size until we have a confirmation of five minutes. Beginner traders may be wise to avoid the one-minute map of trading reversals, and use the five-minute option.

Five Minute Entry

The entry period of five minutes is very easy. Confirmation of Reversal is a candle over candle trend on the 5 minute map. When we have a candle on the five-minute map outside the Bollinger bands, I use that candle's bottom as my switch, and the top of that candle as either my entry point or my double-up. I can take the trade only if the 9 EMA still has 30 cents of profit potential, using the five-minute map. If I already have a half-sized position based on a one-minute chart, I'll double on a confirmation of five minutes. I'm increasing my risk by doubling my position, which means I need to tighten my stop to either break even or -10 cents. Watching the one-minute chart when you enter a reversal of the five minute is important. If the five minute map has already included five consecutive green candles, there is a chance that you may be pursuing too much of the turnaround.

Buying the First Pullback of Reversals

One of the safest reversal strategies is the purchase after confirmation of the first pullback. There are occasions where, during a downtrend, the one minute or five minute chart is too choppy to take a position on the first candle and make a new peak. There are 2 choices in this scenario. One is simply passing on the turnaround and hoping for a better opportunity, and that may be a good option for new traders who need greater assurance before joining trades. My favorite strategy is to purchase the first one minute chart pullback or the five minute map. You can see, in AVGO's example, that the one-minute chart shows many one-minute candles reaching a new high. When you made each of those deals, you'd have had four defeats back to back before you found a winner. In the segment where we addressed entries for one minute, we highlighted the importance of at least 5-10 consecutive candles, but AVGO had not. In this kind of situation, I keep reversal stocks on watch and wait for the one-minute or five-minute candle to make a new high (1), then consolidate over the lows showing support was found (2), and finally break the consolidation high (3). At phase (3), I reach with a pause at the bottom of the consolidation. This entry provides the best combination of a close pause, and supports the start of the reversal. In AVGO's example, the point at which we saw the consolidation breakout coincided almost perfectly with the first five minute candle making a new high. AVGO also revealed (3), that the one-minute candle hit the 20 EMA for the first time since the selloff started. I use the same market scanners when I'm searching for pullback possibilities on reverse trades as when I'm hunting for the first one minute or five minute candles to make a new peak.

Profit Targets

Reversal trading have obvious targets for profits. In fact, reversal trades run back to rational points on the map, unlike a momentum trade that can run and run. I'm looking for reversals to return to the five-minute chart of the 9 EMA. A rapid turnaround could return to the VWAP, and possibly cross the VWAP. Since the 9 EMA is the first benefit goal, I won't take a trade if I can't get a profit loss ratio of at least 2:1, based on an exit at the 9 EMA.

Exit Indicators

1. I placed my stop either at the high of the day or low of the day when I started a reversal trade first. When my stop is hit I'm out of the trade instantly.

2. If the price hits the 9 EMA on the five minute map, or if I reach my 2:1 income loss ratio, I can sell the part. Next, I change my stop to match breakeven.

3. I'll move my stop to the other side of the 9 EMA once the price breaks, and keep adjusting it every 5-10 minutes.

4. I will be doing another partial sale at the VWAP and holding a smaller spot for moving back over the VWAP and for a potential swing trade.

I'm pretty fast exiting reversal trades when they don't look strong. Occasionally I can leap out of them too soon, if anything. One of the things I've found is that with reversal transactions, as we're anticipating the rubber band snap back effect, it's almost instantly needed to happen. The stock may not turn toward me but it's a big warning sign that it's not moving up. As with my momentum trades, my better reversal trades typically work nearly immediately. Reversal trades often stop close to the high or low, before making a big move and heading in the direction of the cycle. Instead of holding out hope that perhaps the turnaround will succeed, that ensures it is much easier to get out of breakeven, or for a small loss, instead of feeling the agony of it tearing against you.

By jumping in for a momentum trade, I'll warn you against the bad habit of covering up a reversal position and flipping directions. Reversal setups are rarely installation dynamics. These are configurations for reversal, because they are comprehensive. Which ensures they are in an incredibly extended position even if they go a further 50 cents and the turnaround will arrive sooner or later. Trading the pattern when extending the' rubber band' is asking for trouble. You'll feel extremely annoyed if you bail out of the reversal spot, hop into the momentum and then the snap back occurs and you fail on both hands. Whenever I get stopped on my first attempt at a reversal, I just wait for a better chance of reversal. If the stock continues to run, this ensures the expansion will be higher, and the opportunity for snapback will also be greater.

CHAPTER 8: STOCK SCANNING AND BUILDING A WATCH LIST

On one of my stock scanners, I found almost any single trade setup. I use the Trade-Ideas portfolio analysis app (www.trade-ideas.com). I can't talk their devices big enough. I will miss out as a dealer without their scanning tools. A trader may have all the market knowledge of the textbooks, but if they can't find real-time configurations, they'll never be successful. Stock scanners are the devices that we use to search for tradable setups. Before stock scanners existed, traders would either trade off a master watch list of their top 50 stocks, or wait for news about a particular stock to break over the wire. This is not an efficient day-trading strategy because out of the many thousand stocks eligible for trade, usually only 5-10 stocks are in operation every day. I find a stock in play with a good trigger if it rises up or down more than 4 percent. Using stock scanners, I will pick the particular type of product I want to see and filter all the noise out. That brings considerable consistency to the process of selecting my stock. I can also make complex scanners to look for unique chart patterns, or I can use basic scanners to check for large matches including stocks that only reported earnings in the last 24hrs.

Full Scanner Layout by Trade-Ideas

Day trading is a very tough profession which we can render with the best tools a little easier. Which involves scanners on property. The opportunity to display historical data from a stock analysis is one of the great features of Trade-Ideas. I will look back and see all the day or week updates, and check the tests. This saves us a tremendous amount of time to sit and watch scans in real-time to develop a history of back checks. We will check back instantly and fix errors or false warning issues easily. I provide the patented stock scanner settings that I developed over the years to all the students in our live trading courses. Students are able to discover occupations using the very same methods that I use every day. Although I have around 15 scanners that I use regularly every day, they are grouped in two categories. I have scanners looking for opportunities for reversal and I have scanners hunting for the leverage markets. These are the two methods that I swap, and these are the things that I need to pursue in real time. All the stock scanners I use is highly tailored to send me a watch list of the sort of product I have the highest percentage of performance selling.

Gap Scanners

The first thing I do each morning is test my scanner for difference. It tells me more than 4 percent of the stock list gapping up or down. I sort the results by the biggest percentage of gap on the gap scanners, then by the largest volume. Every morning I switch on sorting methods to find the most active stocks. We have to monitor the demand as traders so I always put special focus on the sum of pre-market volume.

Creating your Pre-Market Watch List

It's important for your future as a broker, because every day you can create a watch list. Your watch list will be a daily list of the top 4-6 stocks with the potential to make intraday movements of 5-10 percent. Around 9 AM, I've put together a watch list of the top 4-6 companies that I expect will be in action every day. Because of a spark these will be companies still traded on high pre-market volume. I identify such stocks utilizing basic stock scanners that are shown in the chat room of our day. I take notes on the spark, float, key price rates on the daily chart that are in operation and possible entry points for each of the inventories on my watch list. It's important to keep a close eye on the stocks that you put on your daily watch list, because you know you won't miss it if a pattern forms. During the day, many new students jump from chart to chart, and end up missing all the setups because they never concentrated on one stock long enough to see a pattern. Checking at other products on a separate screen, the best approach is to have your preferred watch list stocks on the monitor for the whole day.

Once you get used to creating a watch list of inventories every day, you're well on your way to becoming a trader! You need to consider inventories worth selling in order to trade. It means creating a watch list every day, and then evaluating how each stock operated off your watch list. Occasionally, because of a strong morning sell off, a great looking pre-market nominee will end up out of reach. Many days a product that hasn't been on your watch list at all will become the day's greatest mover.

Momentum Scanners

In search for trend securities, I use that same method in compose a scanner. The critical indicator for momentum stocks is the large relative price and the market increase of 15 minutes. I can see the most popular stocks on the exchange every day by turning up certain limited filters. Both scanners generate any false alerts which is why we can not transact on the basis of a stock scanner's warnings alone. I've got momentum scanners searching for stocks at 52 week highs, regular chart breakouts, huge intraday volume and significant shift pace. Whenever I see a stock showing on one of my momentum scanners, I will immediately start revising the windows and triggers map and search for a Momentum Trading Strategy system to implement.

Some of the strongest warnings for the momentum scanner will be stocks not even on our watch list, which was based on premarket price. Breaking news out in the middle of the day can trigger a stock to come into play unexpectedly. If this is the case, we will carry out a quick analysis of the trigger and the level of risk involved in the trade. Taking a midday trade randomly will lead to unexpected losses if we don't consider the risk first. Each time a stock starts spiking or moving quickly on breaking news, I like following it and making the dust settle before doing any trades. Occasionally prices spike up and then in a matter of minutes come back straight down. If the news is real, and the stock proceeds to sell on heavy volume, subscribing to the watch list is worthwhile. Keep in mind that verifying the origins of any breaking news story is critical before joining a trade. In crack news configurations we should add the Momentum Trading Strategy and probably the Reversal Trading Strategies. Usually, stocks that jump up on news in the middle of the day are worth watching the rest of the day because they are going to trade on high relative value.

Reversal Scanners

I write a stock scanner to look for a specific type of setup. Which means I need to analyze the configuration to appreciate all of its unique features. I set a minimum volume filter of 500,000 shares for reversal transactions, a quality filter of $15-250 and a sequential candle filter of at least 4 (consecutive rising candles). I realize such features are rising to the strongest reversal trades. Instead I start adding RSI (Relative Strength Index) parameters, Bollinger band location and the percentage of change today. After the settings have been finely tuned, the end result is a scanner that shows me stocks at any given time of day, matching my exact entry conditions for a reversal trade.

CHAPTER 9: THE TEN POWER PRINCIPLES: MAKING SURE YOUR TRADING PLAN WORKS

Having a business plan is like having a solid blueprint to build your home, or having a map when you travel to a new place. You already know that without a good business plan a skilled trader will not succeed in the markets.

You learned in the previous step:

- How to identify your goals for finance and trading.
- How to choose the right market for your company goals.
- What timeframe will you trade in.
- Different styles of trading and finding the right one for you.
- How to create a basic plan for the trade

Now that you have established your goals and developed your business plan, you need to make sure it does work. Everything might look great so far, but how can you be sure when you start trading it with real money that the program will work?

It's easier to evaluate a trade policy than you would think. **You'll find 10 Principles of Successful Trading Strategies in this chapter** that we've built and refined over the past few years.

You should use these Power Principles to evaluate your trading strategy, whether you developed it on your own or are thinking about purchasing one. You can dramatically increase your chances of success by checking out a strategy against these principles.

PRINCIPLE #1: USE FEW RULES – MAKE IT EASY TO UNDERSTAND

It may shock you that there are less than ten rules for best trading systems. The more rules you have, the more likely you have "curve-fitted" your trading strategy to past data and such an over-optimized scheme is very unlikely to yield real-market gains.

It's important you understand and execute your rules easily. Markets can act very predictably and move very quickly, so you won't have time to analyze complex formulas to make a decision on trade. Think of effective floor traders: a calculator is the only device they use and they earn thousands of dollars every day.

Example: take a look at the trading approaches in the "Popular Trading Approaches" section. The easy rules are: buy when the RSI drops below 20, or sell when prices move above the upper Bollinger Band.

Consider a trading strategy that has an entry rule like this:

 Buy when the RSI is below 20, and the ADX is between 7 and 12, and the 7-bar moving average is more than 45 degrees, and there is a correlation between the price bars and the MACD, and, and...

Do you really think you should follow this strategy when watching the LIVE markets?

PRINCIPLE #2: TRADE IN ELECTRONIC AND LIQUID MARKETS

I strongly recommend that you trade in electronic markets, because commissions are lower and you get instant fills. You need to know as quickly as possible whether your order has been filled out and at what price, and based on this detail, you schedule your exit.

You should never place an order for exit before you know your order for entry is filled out. If you trade open (non-electronic) outcry markets, you may have to wait a while before getting your fill. By then, the market may already have turned and your profitable trade has turned into a loss!

You obtain your fills in less than a second while trading electronic markets, and can position your exit orders immediately. Trading liquid markets means you can save hundreds or even thousands of dollars from slippage.

Luckily, there are now more and more electronically traded markets. The recent addition of the grain futures markets in the summer of 2006 was a huge success: the volume traded in the electronic contracts surpassed the amount exchanged on the pit markets in January of 2007. The pit-traded maize contract had exchanged 621,800 contracts in December 2007, while the electronic maize contract had a trading volume of 2,444,400 contracts. Some futures markets, all forex currency pairs, and the largest U.S. stock markets are electronically traded. So why would you even want to trade Lumber or Pork Bellies?

PRINCIPLE #3: HAVING LACK OF REALISTIC EXPECTATIONS IS PART OF OUR BUSINESS

A trading system that has no losses is "too good to be true." Recently, I stumbled into a trading system that had a whopping 91 percent winning percentage and a $500 drawdown. WOW!

However, when I looked at the data, it turned out that the system was only being tested on 87 trades and–of course–curve-fitted. If you're going through a trading system of numbers that are too good to be true, then it's probably just that: too good to be true.

Typically the following can be extracted from a robust trading system: a winning percentage of 60-80 percent A benefit factor of 1.3-2.5 A cumulative drawdown of 10-20 percent of the annual profit Use these figures as a rough guideline and you can easily identify curve-fitted systems.

PRINCIPLE #4: MAINTAIN A HEALTHY BALANCE BETWEEN RISK AND REWARD

Let me give you an example: if you go to a casino and gamble all you have on "gold," then you have a 49 percent chance to double your money and a 51 percent chance to lose it all. The same applies to trading: if you gamble a lot, you can make a lot of money, but if you do, there is also a high risk of disaster. You need to strike a good balance between risk and reward.

Make sure you use small stop losses in your trading strategy and that your profit targets are greater than your stop losses.

Stay away from strategies that have a tiny profit target of just $100 and a $2,000 stop loss. The winning percentage will certainly be fantastic, but 2-3 losses in a row can wipe your trading account off.

The perfect balance between risk and reward is 1:1.5 or more-i.e. you should be able to make at least $1.50 for every dollar you risk.

To put it another way, if you apply a $100 stop loss, your profit target should be at least $150.

PRINCIPLE #5: FIND A SYSTEM THAT PRODUCES AT LEAST FIVE TRADES PER WEEK

The higher the volume of your trading, the lower the odds of a month losing. If you have a trading strategy that has a winning percentage-age 70 percent, but produces only one trading per month, then one loser is sufficient to lose a month. In this case, you might have several months to lose in a row before you finally make money.

Which way do you pay your bills meanwhile?

If your trading strategy generates five trades a week then you has 20 trades a month on average. If you have a 70 per cent winning percentage, then your winning month chances are extremely high. And all traders have that goal: to have as many winning months as possible!

PRINCIPLE #6: START SMALL–GROW BIG

Your system of trading will allow you to start small and grow large. A good trading system allows you to start with one or two contracts as your trading account increases.

This compares with many "martingale" trading systems, which involve growing place sizes when you're in a streak of losing.

Perhaps you've heard of this strategy: double your contracts any time you lose, and one winner will win all the money you've expected lost.

Seeing 4-5 losing trades in a row is not uncommon and this strategy would already allow you to trade 16 contracts, or 1,600 shares, of a stock after just 4 losses! If you're trading the E-mini S&P, you'd need at least $63,200 of account size, just to meet the margin requirements. So, if we say you're trading stocks about $100 (e.g., IBM or Apple), then your account would need $160,000.

Now, you may wonder how likely this kind of scenario really is. Response: Quite likely. That was the whole point of the previous few pages. Just think back with the coins to the example: an atypical negative trading run may and does occur.

That's why I don't suggest doubling after every loss. When we trade in a controlled, systematic way, then at the end of the game we will still be in the game when our atypical run occurs.

There will be times when you have losses, or even a series of losses, irrespective of the technique or process you use to trade. It's important to have confidence in your trading plan when these happen; don't try to double your trades to "catch up" on your wins.

The main point I want to make here is that when it has more losses than gains, any trading system you find must move through times.

This is to be expected and it's where effective management of money comes in.

PRINCIPLE #7: AUTOMATE YOUR EXITS

The most common mistakes that traders make, are emotions and human errors. These mistakes must be avoided by any means necessary, especially when the market is starting to move quickly. Panic and indecision may be felt, but if you give in to those feelings, you will suffer a much greater loss than you originally planned. The exit points should be easy to identify. Using "bracket orders" is the best solution for your exit points. Many trading platforms offer bracket orders, which allow you to add a profit target and a stop loss to your entry. You can place your trade on autopilot this way, and the trading system closes your position at the specified rate.

It of course, means you have rules for exiting quickly. Within today's trading platforms, a stop loss of $100 or 1 percent of the entry price can be easily defined.

Exit rules such as "2/3 of the past 5 trading days ' average true size" are more difficult to implement. You should keep your dealing as simple as possible in the beginning.

If you can't make money with easy entry and exit points, with more complicated trading rules, you won't be able to make money. When you can't drive a Ford, you're certainly not going to be able to drive a Ferrari.

PRINCIPLE #8: HAVE A HIGH PERCENTAGE OF WINNING TRADES

Your business strategy will yield more winners than 50%. There's no doubt that trading strategies can also be profitable with smaller winning percentages, but the psychological pressure is huge.

It takes a lot of discipline to take 7 losers out of 10 trades and not to question the program, and many traders can't stand the pressure. They'll start "improving" the plan after the sixth loser, or avoid totally trading it. Gaining confidence in their trading is very beneficial for beginning or beginner traders, and if your strategy gives you a high winning percentage, let's say over 65 percent, your faith will certainly be on the rise.

PRINCIPLE #9: TEST YOUR STRATEGY ON AT LEAST 200 TRADES

The more back-testing trades you use (without curve-fitting), the higher the probability that your trading strategy will succeed in the future.

The more trades you have in your back-test, the lower the margin of error, and the higher the chance of future profit-making.

For a valid performance report you need a minimum of 40 trades. As you can see from the above table, 200 trades are optimal, as the margin of error decreases rapidly from 14 per cent to 7 per cent with only 150 trades added.

The margin of error decreases at a slower rate if you check the program on more than 200 trades. The next 100 trades are only 2 per cent more trust.

PRINCIPLE #10: CHOOSE A VALID BACK-TESTING PERIOD

Recently I saw the following advertisement:' *Since 1994, I have taught thousands of traders worldwide a simple and reliable e-mini trading methodology.*' That's a very interesting claim... The E-mini S&P was introduced in September 1997 and the E-mini NASDAQ was introduced in June 1999; therefore, NONE of those contracts existed until 1997.

Regardless, though, we only need to think about the back-testing period of the contracts. So, if you're designing an E-mini S&P trading strategy, you should just check it back for the past 3-4 years anyway. This is because, although the contract has existed since 1997, practically nobody traded it:

The same is true for the grain futures strategies: they were launched in August 2006. Do not make the mistake of going back on the pit contract to test your trading strategy. When futures contracts start trading electronically, they attract a different kind of trader than their pit-traded counterparts; thus the characteristics of the two markets can be very, very different.

It would be nonsense to think that once they can be traded electronically, the markets will remain the same. Faster fills and lower commissions allow a different kind of trading strategy, and the markets WILL behave differently from the times when they were only traded by pit traders.

CHAPTER 10: THE SECRETS TO DAY TRADING SUCCESS

There's more To Trading than Just Having a Strategy

You understand that one of the single most important factors when it comes to your trade is a good trading strategy.

You'll have a map for your future trading with a proven, reliable strategy, and a guideline for your success. You're going to got a plan. Believe me, most traders just open a trading account out there and start trading, with no idea as to what they're getting into. Just a few of them have a trading strategy and many of them struggle because of that.

The vast majority of them actually fail. A paper from the North American Association of Securities Administrators (NASAA) states:

"Just 11.5 percent [of traders] could exchange [markets] profitably. At least 70 percent of traders are losing money in the markets... 70 percent of the pub-not only will license traders lose, but they will almost certainly lose all they invest"

We would lose at least 70 per cent of everything we spend. And actually just 11.5 percent of the traders would succeed. That is just over 1 in 10. Not huge chances.

But if you have followed the action items described throughout the preceding chapters, then you should have worked out a trading strategy. And, if you do, that small step has dramatically increased the odds of belonging to the 11.5 percent of active out there traders who actually make money.

But here's the trade strategies thing: they're a dime a dozen.

You can find hundreds of books with different trading strategies these days, along with endless web sites offering free trading strategies. In fact, every couple of weeks you'll find "the month's trading strategy" in almost every trade industry journal out there.

So, if so many trading strategies are available, why are only 11.5 per cent of traders making money?

The problem is tactics aren't making a good trader.

There's more that just using a plan to trade. Only time, information, experience and encouragement will turn you into the trader you want to be.

The Ralph Vince Experiment

Ralph Vince is a known and acknowledged financial investor and educator. He's published a number of trading and trading books, and he's also done a very famous experiment called the Ralph Vince Experiment.

Mr. Vince took 40 Ph. D.s and set them up for a computer game to trade in. Now, all of these 40 people had doctorates, but Mr. Vince assured that none of their doctorates had any kind of experience in statistics or trade. Each of them won $1,000 and 100 trades in the game, with a winning percentage of 60 per cent. They earned the amount of money they lost when they won. They lost the amount of money which they sacrificed when they lost Just easy as you can see, they all had a competitive trading strategy.

So, after all the 40's finished their 100 trades, how many do you think they made money?

2. Only 2 out of 40 doctorates have managed to make money. The other 38 weren't good.

Source: journal CSI News, March 1992

The statistics are pretty compelling. Applicants lost 95 per cent. And why, then? And they fell into the age-old traps: poor management of money, fallacy of gamblers and lack of discipline, direction and experience.

Have they built a competitive trading strategy? Needless to say!

Note, with a 60 per cent winning percentage each of the traders took 100 trades. Mr. Vince gave them a lucrative trading strategy to use, but they could still not be successful.

So, there certainly seems to be more to trading than just having a strategy. And that's exactly what you're going to hear about in this section of the book: The other variables involved in your trading performance.

The Seven Mistakes of Traders and How to Avoid Them

So, let's take a look at why traders struggle. Once you know the trading pitfalls, so avoiding them will become easier. In this chapter, we're going to talk about the errors that traders make and how you can prevent them.

First of all, there are two types of errors a trader can make:

The small ones

The big ones

Yes, you're definitely going to make minor mistakes along the way-I guarantee that. When you intended to sell it, you might buy a security, simply because you pushed the wrong button. Or you might buy the wrong stock, just because when you enter the symbol, there's a typo. Another possibility is to place the wrong order, as you enter a $213.5 purchase order instead of $21.35. All of us have had these kinds of things happened.

These are minor errors and they're "forgivable." You might even be able to take advantage of them with a little bit of luck.

Nonetheless, if you are going to be a successful trader, there are big mistakes that you simply must stop.

One of the biggest trading errors you could ever make, for example, is trying to learn and understand everything about trading... and then never actually starting to trade.

I know many aspiring traders who have read countless books, developed dozens of trading strategies, and analyzed a number of markets; but when it comes to real trading, they have failed to pull the trigger. As you know, your knowledge and your experience are a part of your education. If you want to make money from trading, you have to take the plunge and get started eventually.

Yeah, I know: there is a risk that you will lose some money. It is true. You take a risk, when you trade.

What Exactly Is "Risk?"

Risk means "not having control."

Example: When you drive a car on the highway, you're in danger. It is just as plain as this. Yet, luckily, there are certain things we can do to manage this risk: omitting all motorists to have a formal education and performance testing their driving skills absolutely before they are allowed to drive a vehicle. This qualifying process is called acquiring a driver's license.

Automobiles are fitted with certain safety features, such as seat belts, airbags, and anti-brake systems and, let's not forget, a steering wheel that helps you to maneuver around obstacles along the way.

Usually you practice with another per-son (e.g. your parent) when you are new to driving in an empty parking lot BEFORE you hit the road. You start driving at 10 mph, and then you can slowly increase the speed as you become more comfortable. You will most likely leave the parking lot for the open road when you are comfortable in your abilities (but let's not move too fast—perhaps a country road, without traffic!)

All of these things help you to control the risk when driving. You are never going to be able to fully eliminate the risk, but you can take appropriate action to will it.

The same principles apply to trading:

Before you start trading, you should have a formal education and prove your skills. Sadly, before you can open a brokerage account, there are no tests needed, but you should take the time to learn about the markets and develop a strategy before you "hit the open road." Either way, you should add those "security features" while trading.

You should first trade in paper when you're new to trading (see page 235). You can then start trading with one lot / contract, or 100 shares, after you've built up some confidence. You will increase the contract or share size if you are confident and you produce acceptable results.

And you can't afford to lose ever to trade with capital. First get your current financial situation in order, and start trading on then.

Get your credit cleaned up, pay off high interest loans and credit cards, and save on living expenses for at least three months. Once this is done, you're happy to let the money work for you.

Don't sell fast to get rich.

That is the number one concept for managing your risk.

If day trading were quick, everybody in the world would do the same thing: trading every day like mad and becoming wickedly rich at nightfall!

THE TRADER'S PSYCHE

You know you have to have a strategy. And you know there's more to commerce than just a strategy. You heard about the major mistakes that traders make in the previous chapter, and you learned that your biggest enemy is not another investor, or market maker, or broker-it's you.

And because of your feelings, you are your biggest enemy.

You'll find out about the mentality and psychology of successful traders in this chapter. Using a competitive trading strategy AND the right attitude will propel you into the 11.5 percent of the successful traders we've talked about before.

You need to know what to expect while trading on a day to develop the right mindset.

Most traders mistakenly believe that trading, like having an ATM in their front yard, would result in a consistently rising account balance.

But you know already that losses are a part of our trading business. There will be a few days and weeks when your trading meets your expectations, and there will be periods when your trading results are far worse than you would expect.

It's important you have a long-term outlook.

Trading by day means playing a game of numbers. You already know you need to place at least 40 trades before you can look into the strategy's performance. Most traders rate their success only once a month,

Trying to have the maximum number of productive months. Hedge funds measure success periodically or annually.

Long-term assessments have their place, but if you look at your trading results on a daily basis, it will drive you insane. That's why we define goals of the week.

Sure no one wants to go through a drawdown. But it is unavoidable when you trade. The key to that is how you handle it.

Market Wizards: Interviews with Top Traders, the famous Richard Dennis said in an interview with Jack D. Schwager for his book:

"It's totally counterproductive to get caught up in the results. You've got to keep your balance. Getting mentally deflated will mean lacking confidence in what I'm doing. I'm avoiding that because I've always thought it's wrong to concentrate on short-term performance."

And far too many traders depend on outcomes in the short term yet lose their perspective. That's why they're failing: they're going through a loss or a poor week and so they're trying to pursue a different strategy. And while the trading strategy they've just abandoned recovers from the drawdown, the new trading strategy may result in even more losses, so they start looking for another one again.

It's like a dog chasing too many rabbits: he's totally exhausted at the end of the day and he has absolutely nothing to show for it, because he hasn't catches one thing.

Trading during the day includes careful, wise, and cautious trading methods. Successful day traders are cautious, and when trading the stock, do not go overboard. We focus on the quality, not the amount, of every exchange.

Here are some key features of successful traders:

Successful traders are not to blame. We accept and do not dwell on the disadvantages we have, or blame other people or circumstances.

They learn from their mistakes, and continue their business.
Has a system for successful traders. They stick closely to their trading system.
Have experience from successful traders. They know most jobs aren't going to be lucrative the minute they open.
It is not over trade that effective traders do. We understand that over-trading puts their portfolio in jeopardy and we know that not every day is a trading day. They wait for openings with high probability.

Successful traders realize nothing is foolproof at 100 per cent. We have faith in their metrics, but are mindful of other factors that may affect their trade.

Successful traders are not being left in a losing trade. They respect the stop losses they set, and they don't keep their position in the hopes that the market will eventually "go their way." We take their time to choose trades, and they are picky about what trades to jump on. They don't place orders just for the sake of every second getting a position in the market.

Successful traders are clinging to a successful strategy. They have one or three really good strategies and they use them over and over and over again.

Successful traders have the adaptability. Their trading methods and decisions are adjusted to changing market conditions.

Successful traders understand what kind of trader they are. We are not pressuring them to compete with methods or tactics which do not suit their personality.

Successful traders tend to rely on steady earnings. You know that a sure way to lose money is to disregard small-profit trades and angling for a "grand slam."

Successful traders act. They are not allowing their fear to control their decisions or to interfere with their trade.

Growing traders use systems which are growing. Their trading methods and indicators focus on high-probability trades, sound money management, keeping their strategies free of curve-fit-ting, and working their system into their successful implementation business plans.

Successful traders acknowledge "good" commerce. They do not base their assessment on profit or loss; they base it on whether or not they have followed their business plan to the letter. Even if they DID lose money, it is a "healthy" trade so long as they stick to their strategy.

Successful traders are taking some time off. They realize the importance of taking breaks to clear their heads from trading and the markets.

Successful traders are unafraid of losses. We know that, and expect them; losses are part of their business.

If you are in a position to adopt the right psychological mindset, you will gain a significant edge in the market.

I can't stress this enough: One of the keys to investment success is the right mindset, and most traders don't realize this.

Greed and Fear

Two emotions are constantly present in day-trading: greed and fear. If your trade goes well, your natural inclination is to trade even more, opening up to substantial losses. And if your trade goes wrong, then you will be plagued by terror. Fear of loss or fear of further loss is scaring traders.

Greed and fear are negative feelings, and are affected by all traders; they are a natural part of the psychology of every trader. Greed and fear can irrationally cause traders to act: they may know what they should do, but they simply cannot.

The bottom line: if you're afraid or greedy, and when trading day you can't control your feelings, then you're going to have a very hard time profiting.

But when you trade well, you'll have a fantastic chance of success in accordance with your trading plan. Feel proud of yourself for good business and decision-making, but don't dwell on it or allow arrogance to take hold. Keep your head up and keep applying a sound trading strategy, even if you suffer losses remember, they're just a part of the business.

Do not allow you to get caught up in positive or negative feelings—consider the trading psychology and realize that there is no guarantee of trade.

Work toward your state of mind. If a trade goes wrong, then try to find out why it did, and learn from it. The only way to overcome negative feelings is to execute a trading system with discipline. Whether you're a day trader or an investor, and whether you're investing in commodities, securities, or currencies, the truth is that your market psychology can affect the outcomes.

Without a solid reason you should never trade. Don't run the market down. If a market is moving rapidly but you are not taking part in this move because your entry criteria have not been met, don't worry. When you miss a deal, there's another just around the corner. Practice patience, and exercise discipline.

You need to have a clear plan to follow to control your emotions. It is just as critical to have the proper trading psychology as having a reliable trading strategy.

The more you are mentally prepared for the trade, the more you are going to trade. Remember my focus on trading well, not on winning more. Profits don't define a good day in day-trading. Successful day traders define a good day as one that is studied and prepared and that follows the overall strategy of their trade.

THE THREE "SECRETS" TO DAY TRADING SUCCESS

Trading can be easy but it isn't easy. And if you exacerbate that, trading is definitely more difficult. Remember the saying: "A Confused Mind Takes No Action." As an investor, every single day you MUST take action, so you must avoid confusion. So just keep it quick. Very straight forward. Here are the three "Secrets" to Day Trading Success

Secret 1: Trading In the Right Direction

You will buy when the market is the and selling when the market is down. That's how they make money.

Secret 2: Always Know When to Exit A Trade

It is important that you know when to exit with a benefit AND when to exit with a loss.

Secret 3: Trade in the Right Market

A developing market is the right one. If you know, if you trade a developing market, money is made in movements–either up or down–so you're significantly in improving your chances of making money.

Now you know why I put in quotation marks the word "secrets." These are by no means "secrets." Alas, most traders do not realize the importance of these realities and tend to forget them.

Losing traders focus on finding a "magic trading tool," visiting countless websites and investing hundreds and thousands of dollars on books, courses and software packages.

Don't make exactly the same mistake. Keep it simple to sell.

Note, today's trade performance "secrets" are common. These are applicable to any market, whether you trade stocks, futures, options, or forex. And they apply to every timeline, which is why they are so strong.

Focus on the "secrets:"

1.) Learn how to assess if the market is rising or falling.

2.) Know when to get out of business, when to make a profit and when to bail if the economy does not move in your favor.

3.) And learn how to get the market right.

Don't make it too hard to trade. Stick to fundamentals. When you can't drive a Chevrolet, you can't drive a Ferrari, as you already know. And if at 10 mph you can't drive a car, you shouldn't try driving it at 80 mph.

Remember the Principle of Power #1: Use Few Rules make It Easy to understand that's how it should be your business plan.

The Tenets of Day Trading

You've learned a lot throughout the course of this book, and you should be well on your way to becoming a good day trader. You'll find a review of the most critical tenets of trade performance in this chapter.

Online day-trading requires patience as well as practicality. To be successful-fulfill, you have to focus on your trading technique, not your trading frequency. Note, on quantity, price! In online trading there are many factors which play a vital role.

Initially, people don't start with specific goals. Many companies are entering markets and have no idea what they're trying to do. The first rule is that you know what you're trying to achieve. That's your strategy for business.

Look at the following-my list of basic day trading tenets.

Understand the Risk

The market for online trading can be volatile, which creates risk. To be successful, you need to be aware of factors that can influence prices, such as economic releases, earning reports and government officials statements. Staying up-to-date with new developments will allow you to make sounder business decisions.

Choose a Trading Time

Before you reach the online trading market, be sure to pick a time frame that fits your lifestyle. There's no point trying to trade if you can't find an appropriate time to do it. Everyone has obligations in their lives that can't be ignored, so you have to determine for yourself which block of time you're more comfortable with is regularly scheduled.

Build Your Day Trading Strategy

Every online day trader should have an online trading strategy that he practices diligently. Most of these techniques will have common elements, including signaling instructions, markers, and entry and exit rules. Determine your plan before you start trading.

Right-Market Trading

Different markets have different trading profiles that vary in volatility (the online currency market is considered to be the most volatile). Some are suitable for intraday trading while others are propitious for long-term action. Determine the market you want to invest in based on factors such as size of your portfolio, timeline for trading, professional know-how and risk tolerance.

Be Open to Learning

There are ranges of risk-free ways for you to gain experience when you're a first-time day trader on the market. For example, you can practice your order execution and trading systems with a demo account to check their viability before putting your actual money into the stake. Use the ample resources available to learn and practice online day trading craftsmanship.

Don't trade too often

Over-trading is one of the traders ' most common mistakes. This happens mainly when traders try to compensate with' only a few more trades' for their previous losses. Wise traders may encourage themselves after a loss to pause from trading activity, rather than selling frenziedly in an attempt to recover their profits.

Starting Small

Starting small is a wise choice, particularly if you're quite new to day trading online. Being cautious in your trade decisions helps protect you from possible errors and failures. Remember, if you trade big, you lose big money and you're setting up for big failure.

Remember also some of these popular day trading strategies to stick to:

Trust in the day trading system that you are pursuing. If and until you have thoroughly investigated all of its trading options, don't question the effectiveness of its rules and methods. Trade just twice a day—once in the morning and once in the evening. Continue to trade in this way for the first 2 to 3 months at least. A conservative timetable will save you from the over-trading temptation.

Make a $250 or $300 profit per contract per week target.

You will turn off your trading screen and take a break until the following Monday when you get a good trade and hit the weekly goal of $250 or more. This is going to be good for your health—and it will help prevent overtrading too. Trust me, when the discipline you've learned with a small weekly target is extended to a larger weekly goal (where you're trying to sell 10-20 contracts), you're going to be very happy you've taken the time to work on the smaller goal first.

If you cannot achieve your set income target in a given week for whatever reason, don't worry. Everybody has been through it. Just concentrate on consistent results in your trading and you'll find success.

CHAPTER 11: THREE STEP DAY TRADING PLAN

We place our students on a three-step trading plan in our live trading classes, and work with them twice a week to check their growth. It is extremely important that students transact in their first months of trading in a virtual and closely monitored environment. We want to see the errors our students make, so we can fix them easily and change the bad habits. Both students learn to swap errors. That is a part of the process of thinking. We have students trading in a simulated environment, so there's no price tag attached for their eventual loses and novice mistakes. Many students will also learn during the first few months of trading that the level of risk involved in day-trading is not ideal for them. We encourage honest reflection of your trading experience. Day trading can be frustrating and it's not for everybody to live with financial loss on an almost daily basis.

The ability to engage in day-to-day trading as the primary source of income, is not a capability acquired overnight. It takes thousands of hours of exercises, preparation and analysis. Mastery comes with time , like almost any other career. The problem for many students is that, in their first few months of investing, they make mistakes, blow up their accounts and give up before they really had a chance to succeed. The inability to manage risk and the propensity to live unproven trading strategies usually lead to blow-ups in the profession. We want to avoid having the painful experience with our graduates. Having a skilled investor who doesn't have a horror story with great losses and big mistakes will be uncommon, we all have them. Often a question of financial resources is the distinction between traders who give up and those who keep fighting on. Our aim is to transact in a simulated environment for you, until you have proven that you can be successful. You will have perfected your strategy by the end of our three-step trading plan and developed a sense of emotional equilibrium that will help you to trade through the ups and downs, without losing focus.

Setting realistic expectations is critical before you launch your trading scheme. Expect that you're unlikely to produce substantial profits in your first six months. Then, you take the necessary steps to lay the foundation for your future growth as a dealer. Most traders may try to miss precautions and end up making expensive mistakes that will threaten their ability to continue trading. Remember, every single trade you take will give you a bit more experience and a better market understanding. That's why the more you will live even in the business break, or just tread water with small profits, the better the chances of success. You have to live until your success.

Three Step Trading Plan You'll start with 30 minutes of aerobic exercise each morning during the first month of our trading plan. You'll be doing it for the next three months, Monday-Friday. Focusing on the mental training needed to make the right decisions under pressure is really necessary for our students and exercise has been proven to help sharpen the mind. As I workout every morning, I tell myself that I am doing this so that I can be the best possible dealer. Bearing in mind the bigger picture helps the exercise move smoother.

Once you've finished your exercise, the first thing you'll do when you're sitting down at your office is glance at the gap check for the largest gappers to start making a 4-6 stock watch list. The news trigger correlated with each stock and the admission rates will be written down, and transactions will be halted. If you're in our chat room for the day, you'll see the breaking news updates for all the major changing stocks. The headlines for all the gappers are typically posted by 9 AM. Around 9:15 AM you should check your watch list. This will be a list of candidates for Gap and Go, and maybe a few higher priced stocks that will have a strong impetus, but will be too risky for trading in Gap and Go. You will use the order entry time between 9:15 AM and 9:30 AM to submit an order for each of the top four Gap and Go candidates. You'll be setting your entry price based on Gap and Go Trading Policy guidelines. When the market opens, and the trades start firing at the predefined breakout points, all you need to do is push the buy button and start handling your open positions. As the day continues, you can check for trade opportunities on the Momentum Scanners and on the Reversal Scanners.

You'll be taking 10 trades a day during our three Stage Trading Plan. You can take more than 10 trades a few days, while you take fewer other days. The goal is to sell, feel the emotions of being in a role and control the exchange. Your market should be focused on Strategies for Gap and Go, Momentum Trading Strategies, and Strategies for Reversal Trading. It is extremely important in a spreadsheet that you chart any single trade. Throughout our Live Trading Courses, we study our students ' table boards. We want to analyze the level of success, average winners and average losses, and which technique you can sell. Your first month of trading is not about how much money you're made, it's about discovering which tactics work better for your style, and figuring out what kind of trader you're going to be. We'll get you concentrate on the tactics you sold the most during your first month in the second and third months. You need to master one strategy as a day trader. Mastering one strategy will be key to your market survival whilst learning other strategies. Trading day is not a career in which you can excel as a jack of all trades, but as a master of none. For one technique you need to reach a maturity degree before implementing another.

Step 1 in a Virtual Account: First Month

You are going to transact in a simulated environment during your first step. You pay $50 per deal, with a maximum size of 100 shares on stocks over $20, and a maximum size of 200 shares on stocks below $20, respectively. Every day you'll take 10 trades with a 50 per cent success rate target. Using a 2:1 profit Loss ratio, and in your first month you may not even achieve 50 per cent success. We want to be pragmatic and set your goal of everyday income at just $150 a day. This allows for mistakes and accounts for the possibility of small winners, while testing different strategies for success.

You must also follow a daily max loss of $150, with a maximum loss of $50 per trade. That means you'll have to shut down the platform for the day if you hit your full max loss on three consecutive trades. This is a method of enormously important risk management. There's a high likelihood that our trading will become mentally affected after we have reached our peak loss. This also holds true for me. I'm still doing a total defeat, so at the end of the day I walk away. We estimate you to reach your $150 daily target four days out of the week during your first month, month, and one day you'll meet your total loss. Which means your weekly target, compounded by three, or $450 per week, is your average objective. Such daily and weekly goals do not take commissions into consideration, because you trad in a simulated environment.

By the end of your first trading month, you'll need to check your trading numbers. Your percentage of overall success, by plan, by time of day and by price range will be important to note. Your profit-loss figures will also be important to note. If you've been able to trade an average of 10 trades a day, you'll be able to analyze around 200 trades across.

Your first month's performance is measured not by total profits, but by your profit-loss ratio and your progress rate. The big question is, are the numbers you actually have sustainable? Did you manage to cap expenses at no more than $50 per trade? A low percentage of progress is the most popular challenge for our students over the first month. So long as you have a good profit-loss ratio, as you accumulate experience and learn to recognize effective configurations, we will work on improving your performance. If you have achieved Step 1 successfully you will be ready to graduate to the next step. If not, you will carry on the trading plan for the first month until you get better results. Students in our live trading courses meet with us twice a week to assess their growth, address issues and set targets for next trading sessions.

Step 1 in a Live Account - Second Month

Once you've successfully completed a month in the simulated environment, you may consider switching to a live trading account. Many students spend several months in a simulated environment before reaching a level of success they feel justified in a live account trading. It's not a phase that can be hurried into becoming a successful trader.

You'll take the data from your first month to make changes to your policy during your second month of the trading plan. If you find an area of particular weakness, that type of trading will be avoided, whether it's a particular strategy, price range or a certain time of day. Alternatively, we'll let you concentrate on the field where you have potential to demonstrate.

You will replicate phase 1 when you are ready to switch to a Live Trading account. The thing is, you're going to be dealing for real money and you might notice that the feelings of real money trading alter the feeling. This could take some time to acclimatize. Once you have successfully traded in a live trading account for one month, you are ready to graduate from Step 2 of our trading plan.

Step 2 - Third Month

You're going to keep selling on average 10 days a day but now you're going to risk up to $100 per contract. Your maximum size of place is now 200 stock shares above $20 and 400 stock shares below $20. Your daily income goal is 300 dollars and your daily maximum loss is 300 dollars. You have a weekly target of $900, compounded by three times the daily goal.

You should continue your exercise regimen throughout the third month, and keep tracking all your trades in a spreadsheet. You must evaluate your results at the end of the month and make adjustments if appropriate.

Step 3 - Final Month

You will make further changes in your final month of our trading plan based on your preceding month's results. As day traders, we continuously change our strategies and techniques to adapt to evolving markets. Once you've built a level of self-confidence and ability, you'll literally float from one approach to the next, based on higher market conditions. This is the ebb and flow of the economies we will respond to. You'll increase your risk per transaction to $200 for month three. Your maximum position size will be 500 stock shares over $20, and 1000 stock shares under $20, respectively. Your average regular income is $600 a day, with a weekly goal of $1800 a week. Once you've successfully completed our three Phase Trading Plan, you're on track to make a day trader just short of $100,000 annually. This is something of a positive. They teach day-to-day trade skills that can be used to produce revenues. We're not going to tell you that success comes immediately or that in your first year of trading you will earn a million bucks, but our students are demonstrating that achievement is possible for those who strive for it.

CONCLUSION

The frustrating reality I'm sure you know is that most who try won't get success in trading. The odds are stacked against us with just 1 in 10 to survive. We've dealt with the primary reasons most traders fail. We struggle because of a lack of education in the business and a lack of risk control. Such reasons of disappointment are completely avoidable, and you are demonstrating a level of dedication by spending your time reading this book that far exceeds the majority of new traders. It is the same amount of commitment required for success. I have struggled for years to find success as a dealer. I was lucky enough to be able to tread water on the market before I learned. I lived until I prospered. This did not come easily to me, and I had to resolve mental roadblocks over the fear of loss felt by so many traders. I experienced through the lengthy trial and error cycle. I hope I can help by showing you the methods I use every day to save you the agony of that operation. That book is a compilation of my years of market trading. I went through the chaos of 1000-point market crashes and witnessed the sheer thrill of 1000 per cent short squeezes in biotech. One of the biggest things I've discovered through my trading years is never to fear the business.

Each trader is a volume hunter and volatility tracker, and a risk manager. Each new market day poses a whole new set of challenges and growth opportunities. The economy is competitive and the two days are not always the same. I had days in which I earned hundreds of thousands of dollars, and had days in which I gave back three months ' earnings in a matter of minutes. A trader's life is one of highs and downs. Trading is a career that will certainly not bore you, but could overwhelm you if you can not cope with the emotional pressures. I would like to stress the importance of balance in life to all of our students. The best traders develop and sustain strategies to cope with stress, and remember to take the time to get away from the computer screens to enjoy life. We are working hard and we are playing really well. That is a day-trader's career. I hope you'll come along with us.

www.ingramcontent.com/pod-product-compliance
Lightning Source LLC
Chambersburg PA
CBHW030630220526
45463CB00004B/1474